Tribunal of Inquiry
Appointed by instrument of
An Taoiseach
dated the 7th day of February 1997
Sole Member
The Honourable Mr. Justice Brian McCracken

Tribunal Office
State Apartments,
The Upper Yard,
Dublin Castle,
Dublin 2.
Tel: 6705666
Fax: 6705490

25 August 1997

Mr. Bertie Ahern TD
Taoiseach
Government Buildings
Upper Merrion Street
Dublin 2

Dear Taoiseach,

I enclose herewith my Report as Sole Member of the Tribunal appointed by Order made on the 7th day of February 1997 by the then Taoiseach Mr John Bruton, pursuant to resolutions of Dáil Éireann and Seanad Éireann each passed on the 6th day of February 1997 to enquire into payments made to certain politicians or connected persons or political parties by Dunnes Holding Company or any associated enterprises and/or by Mr. Ben Dunne in accordance with the Terms of Reference contained in the said Order.

Yours sincerely

The Honourable Mr.
Justice Brian McCracken

Registrar: Annette O'Connell BL; Solicitor to the Tribunal: John Lawless BCL

iii

14·5

Contents

Chapter 5

Chapter 6

Chapter 7

SCHEDULES

Preface

There has been almost unprecedented media coverage of every aspect of the Tribunal, in the course of which the phrase "the Tribunal team" has been coined. I do not think there could be any better collective description of all the people involved. As Tribunals go, this Tribunal sat to hear evidence for a comparatively small number of days. By far the greater part of the Tribunal's time was taken up with investigative work behind the scenes and with the examination of large numbers of documents. This necessitated team work of the highest order and I have been very fortunate that everybody concerned has worked together and worked for each other as a team, notwithstanding what at times were long and unsociable hours.

Obviously I owe a particular debt to the legal members of the team. Denis McCullough SC, Michael M. Collins SC, Anthony Aston BL, John Lawless, Solicitor, and Joanne Dwyer, Solicitor, were highly professional, dedicated and tireless in both the presentation of evidence and in the lengthy preparatory work.

The Registrar to the Tribunal, Annette O'Connell BL brought to the Tribunal her considerable skills and experience as a High Court Registrar and also was invaluable both in organising the hearings of the Tribunal and ensuring the smooth running and organisation of the Tribunal at all times. Most importantly, she acted as the public face of the Tribunal, and effectively as its public relations officer.

The organisation of the office and of my requirements and those of the legal members of the team fell initially to Eilís de Buitléir, and subsequently to Karl Martin. Both ensured that all needs were catered for promptly and efficiently and that the office functioned smoothly. Karl Martin was able to draw on his experience of having carried out a similar function in relation to the Tribunal of Inquiry into the Blood Transfusion Service Board.

Dave Hayes and Colm Grace looked after the vitally important work of filing and photocopying without which the Tribunal could not have operated. Jacinta Larkin, Marie Heffernan, Sinead Keelan and Annette Butler, before she left to devote her time to motherhood, performed the secretarial and telephone duties speedily and without complaint in spite of the pressures which were present at times.

Finally, mention should be made of Aoife Ní Fhearghaíl, who organised the transcription of the evidence, both in print and on disk, and who provided basic instruction in computers to those who, like myself, were totally computer illiterate.

My thanks also to those who advised and assisted the Tribunal in London and in the Cayman Islands, and in particular to Robert Neill of Herbert Smyth, Solicitors in London, Charles Quin of Quin & Hampson, lawyers in Grand Cayman and Antonio Bueno QC, who gave general advice in both jurisdictions and represented the Tribunal before the Grand Court of the Cayman Islands.

To all of these people, I would give my thanks for making my task easier, in particular through the relaxed, friendly and informal atmosphere which they helped to generate.

The Honourable Mr. Justice Brian McCracken

Chapter 1

Terms of Reference

On the 6th day of February 1997 Resolutions were passed by Dáil Éireann and Seanad Éireann for the establishment of a Tribunal of Inquiry pursuant to the Tribunals of Inquiry (Evidence) Act 1921 (as adapted) and the Tribunals of Inquiry (Evidence) (Amendment) Act 1979. On the 7th day of February 1997 the Taoiseach Mr. John Bruton made the necessary order appointing the Tribunal which order is cited as the Tribunals (Evidence) Acts 1921 and 1979, Order, 1997. The terms of this Order, which include the full terms of the Resolutions of both Houses of the Oireachtas, are set out in the First Schedule to this report. In essence, however, the terms of reference of the Tribunal were

> "to enquire urgently into, and report to the Clerk of the Dáil and make such findings and recommendations as it sees fit, in relation to the following definite matters of urgent public importance:—
>
> (a) all payments in cash or in kind directly or indirectly whether authorised or unauthorised within or without the State which were made to or received by
>
> > (i) persons who were between 1st January 1986 and 31st December, 1996, members of the Houses of the Oireachtas,
> >
> > (ii) their relatives or connected persons as defined in the Ethics in Public Office Act, 1995,
> >
> > (iii) Political parties
> >
> > from Dunnes Holding Company and/or any associated enterprises ... and/or Mr. Ben Dunne or any person on his behalf or any companies trusts or other entities controlled directly or indirectly by Mr. Ben Dunne between 1st January 1986 and 31st December, 1996, and the considerations, motives and circumstances therefor".

The extensive powers of the Tribunals of Inquiry (Evidence) Act 1921 (as adapted) and the Tribunals of Inquiry (Evidence) (Amendment) Act 1979 were available to the Tribunal and it is important to note that these powers were in fact exercised on a number of occasions by the Tribunal.

Chapter 2

Historical Background to the Establishment of the Tribunal of Inquiry

---

Dunnes Stores Group

In 1943 Mr. Bernard Dunne Senior opened a retail premises in Cork City. The business expanded considerably during the 1940s and 1950s and a number of other stores were opened throughout Ireland, all of which were operated on a personal basis by Mr. Bernard Dunne Senior until 1963.

On 30th April 1963 an unlimited company called Dunnes Holding Company was formed and the entire business was transferred to that company. In March 1964 a trust, known as the Dunnes Settlement Trust, was set up to hold the ordinary shares in Dunnes Holding Company, which shares did not have any voting rights. The trust also held thirty two of the one thousand issued preference shares in Dunnes Holding Company, which did have voting rights, while the remaining preference shares were held outside the trust by members of the Dunne family. The trust was a discretionary trust, the purpose of which was to provide for the children and grandchildren of Mr. Bernard Dunne Senior. It was initially set up for a term of 21 years from 16th March 1964. The present trustees of the trust are Mr. Edward Montgomery, Mr. Frank Bowen, Mr. Noel Fox and Mr. Bernard Uniacke.

Mr. Bernard Dunne Senior died in April 1983 and the management of the company was assumed by five of his children. Mr. Ben Dunne and Mr. Frank Dunne became joint managing directors and Mrs. Margaret Heffernan, Mrs. Elizabeth McMahon and Miss Therese Dunne became directors of the company. They were all actively involved in the affairs of the company, and in the ten years after the death of Mr. Bernard Dunne Senior the business experienced significant expansion. While Mr. Frank Dunne was in name a joint managing director, he did not play an active role in the day-to-day running of Dunnes Stores. During this period Mrs. Margaret Heffernan had responsibility for personnel and for ladies underwear, Mrs. Elizabeth McMahon for ladies fashions including the Cassidy Group of stores and Miss Therese Dunne for childrens wear. Mr. Ben Dunne was responsible for the grocery side of the business and for menswear and footwear. He was also in charge of the development of new stores. As will be seen later in this report, the reality is that he had sole and complete control of the financial side of the business

5

during the ten year period from 1983 to 1993 when the turnover of the company rose from about £300 million per annum to about £850 million per annum. It was a growing, thriving and highly successful business.

During this period the business was operated through a number of subsidiary and associated companies, both in Ireland and elsewhere. In particular, there were companies in the Far East involved in the purchase and transport of goods, which companies generated considerable profits. These profits were both made and held outside Ireland. It would appear that these companies did not form part of the Dunnes Stores Group in the legal sense, and they appear to have been almost totally under the control of Mr. Ben Dunne. The Tribunal has not investigated either the legal position of these companies, nor their activities, as this would appear to be outside the Terms of Reference, but the companies have considerable importance in that they were the source of much of the monies with which the Tribunal is concerned.

Disputes within Dunnes Stores Group

For some time prior to February 1992 there had been disagreements within the board of Dunnes Holding Company as to some of the policy decisions and trading methods of Mr. Ben Dunne. Mr. Ben Dunne also had a number of personal problems around this period. In February 1992 he was charged in Florida with possession of cocaine, and after a well publicised trial he was ordered to spend a month in a rehabilitation clinic in England. After this the personal and policy differences on the board became aggravated and in February 1993 Mr. Ben Dunne was removed as Chairman of Dunnes Holding Company, and in July 1993 he was removed as an executive director of the company.

Arising out of these matters, Mr. Ben Dunne issued two sets of proceedings. The first was a petition claiming relief under Section 205 of the Companies Act 1963 on the basis that he was an oppressed shareholder. The second set of proceedings were brought against the Trustees of the Dunnes Settlement Trust claiming certain reliefs against them, and in effect alleging that the trust was a sham. The object of these proceedings would appear to have been to force the other members of his family to acquire his interest in Dunnes Holding Company for as high a price as possible.

Be that as it may, in the course of the proceedings the defendants in the action against the Trustees sought particulars of Mr. Ben Dunne's claim. Among the particulars given were allegations by Mr. Ben Dunne that he had made payments to Mr. Charles Haughey of "£1 million+" between 1988 and 1991 at a time when the latter was Taoiseach. He also alleged that he made payments of some £200,000 to the Fine Gael Party between 1989 and 1992. The relevant extracts from the particulars are set out in the Second Schedule to this report. It subsequently transpired that the amounts and dates given were not in all cases strictly accurate, but they were broadly correct. It should be noted that these allegations were contained in an exchange of correspondence between the solicitors for the various parties, in which particulars were sought and furnished, but this correspondence, being purely communications between the parties, was not placed on the file of the proceedings in the Central Office of the High Court.

In addition, in the course of their preparation for the case, the Dunnes Stores Group instructed a well-known firm of accountants, namely Price Waterhouse, to investigate certain specific accounts which it was alleged were operated solely by Mr. Ben Dunne but which contained monies which were the property of the Group. Price Waterhouse reported on a large number of payments out of these accounts which, it was alleged, had not been authorised by the company. These included payments to Mr. Michael Lowry TD from an account in the Marino Dublin branch of the Bank of Ireland, which account was operated by Mr. Ben Dunne without the knowledge of the board of directors. How this was allowed to happen is outside the scope of this inquiry, but it is acknowledged by all parties that the monies in this account were in fact the property of one or more entities in the Dunnes Stores Group.

Both actions were listed for hearing on 16th November 1994. After considerable negotiations, both actions were settled. Mr. Ben Dunne withdrew all allegations which he had made in the course of the proceedings, and the remaining members of the family acquired his interest in the entire enterprise.

Allegations In Dáil Éireann

As a result of the settlement of the two actions, neither the correspondence containing the particulars set out in the second schedule hereto, nor the Price Waterhouse Report, were ever made public. However, in November 1996 allegations appeared in the media to the effect that the Dunnes Stores Group paid over £200,000 towards the renovation of Mr. Michael Lowry's house at Holy Cross in County Tipperary. At the time of these allegations, Mr. Lowry was Minister for Transport, Energy and Communications, and on 2nd December 1996 he resigned his ministerial post and announced that he would be making a personal statement to Dáil Éireann. Within days further articles appeared in the media, possibly as a result of a leaking of the reply to the above mentioned notice for particulars. These particularly referred to payments of over £1 million allegedly made by Mr. Ben Dunne to a retired politician. There was speculation that the politician might have been Mr. Charles Haughey, the former Taoiseach.

Mr. Michael Lowry ultimately made his promised statement to Dáil Éireann on 19th December 1996, acknowledging that he had received certain payments from the Dunnes Stores Group, and acknowledging that his tax affairs were not in order. The admissions made by him in this statement will be referred to in considerably more detail at a later stage of this report.

In the meantime, in early December 1996, the Committee on Procedure and Privileges appointed retired Judge Gerard Buchanan to report to the Committee in relation to the Price Waterhouse Report on the following terms:

"(a) examine it and extract from the Report details of any payments made to or transactions entered into in relation to Members or former Members of Dáil Éireann or Seanad Éireann, or any Local Authority, Health Board or other similar body, or employees or Board members of public bodies or persons remunerated directly or indirectly out of public funds or to their relatives or to political parties and

(b) report to the Dáil Committee on Procedure and Privileges and to the Seanad Committee on Procedure and Privileges full details of all such payments, transactions and/or references to any such persons or bodies, including in such report full details of any explanations in relation thereto as may be furnished to him by Dunnes Holding Company or such person and any observations or recommendations as he may consider appropriate."

It should be noted that Judge Buchanan was simply reporting on the Price Waterhouse findings, he was not conducting an inquiry, and although he obtained assistance in his examination of the Price Waterhouse Report, he had no power to subpoena witnesses or hold hearings. Furthermore, his examination was limited to payments referred to in the Price Waterhouse Report, which in turn had been limited to the examination of certain accounts only, and not the entirety of the Dunnes Stores accounts, let alone other accounts controlled by Mr. Ben Dunne. On 3rd February 1997 Judge Buchanan submitted an interim report to the Committee on Procedure and Privileges, which disclosed certain payments to Mr. Michael Lowry, together with payments to Mrs. Maureen Haughey, Mr. Ciaran Haughey and Fr. Eoghan Haughey. The report also disclosed a payment of £85,000 to the Fine Gael Party. It was quite clear that, because of the very restricted nature of the investigation, the information was far from complete in relation to payments by the Dunnes Stores Group or any member of the Dunne family to politicians. For example, before Judge Buchanan's report was ever presented, the Fine Gael Party admitted receiving £180,000 from the Dunnes Stores Group or from Mr. Ben Dunne. It should be added, for completeness sake, that on 6th March 1997 Judge Buchanan submitted his final report to the Committee on Procedure and Privileges, which dealt primarily with payments to public officials, and while it did disclose certain further payments to Mr. Michael Lowry, it otherwise added little to the interim report that is relevant to this inquiry. Meanwhile, following receipt of Judge Buchanan's interim report, the Dáil and Seanad decided to set up this Tribunal of Inquiry.

Progress of the Tribunal

Immediately after the establishment of the Tribunal Ms. Annette O'Connell, a Registrar of the High Court, was appointed as Registrar to the Tribunal and Mr. John Lawless, a Solicitor in the Chief State Solicitor's Office, was appointed as Solicitor to the Tribunal. Subsequently, Ms. Joanne Dwyer was seconded from the Chief State Solicitor's Office to act as Assistant Solicitor to the Tribunal. The Tribunal appointed Mr. Denis McCullough SC, Mr. Michael M. Collins SC, and Mr. Anthony Aston BL to be Counsel to the Tribunal.

At this stage no documents or statements were available to the Tribunal other than Judge Buchanan's interim report. The Price Waterhouse Report had only been made available to Judge Buchanan under very strict terms of confidentiality and was not initially available to the Tribunal. The Dunnes Stores Group were understandably concerned that confidential information concerning the affairs of the group might enter into the public domain and after some negotiation with their representatives, and representatives of other interested parties, a formula for preserving the confidentiality of documents submitted to the Tribunal was drawn up in the terms set out in the Third Schedule to this report.

The Tribunal then contacted a number of people who it was considered might be in a position to assist, either by the production of documents or by the making of statements. All known members of the Oireachtas for the relevant period were contacted, and an advertisement was inserted in the press also seeking the assistance of such persons, as the present addresses of all former members were not known. All political parties were also written to, seeking details of any payments made to them which would come within the terms of reference of the Tribunal. The Tribunal is glad to record the co-operation of a large majority of the members of the Oireachtas and of all the political parties due to which a number of payments which will be referred to below were disclosed.

In the request to the Grand Court of the Cayman Islands, it was sought to obtain an order that evidence be taken from and documents produced by the parties set out in the Fifth Schedule hereto. All such parties are present or former employees of Ansbacher Cayman Limited, a bank situated in the Cayman Islands into which the Tribunal had been able to trace certain of the monies paid by Mr. Ben Dunne. The application for letters of request was vigorously opposed by Mr. John Furze, who had at the relevant time been a joint Managing Director of Ansbacher Cayman Limited and was one of the persons from whom it was sought to obtain oral evidence and documents. Ansbacher Cayman Limited and the persons named in the letters of request, other than Mr. John Furze, indicated that they would consider themselves bound by any order made in respect of the opposition by Mr. John Furze, and requested that the Grand Court be so informed by Counsel for the Tribunal. The Tribunal retained Mr. Antonio Bueno QC, who is also a member of the Irish Bar, and Mr. Charles Quin of the firm of Quin & Hampson in Grand Cayman, to represent it. The Tribunal's application was heard in the Grand Court of the Cayman Islands on 22nd, 23rd and 27th May 1997 before Mr. Justice Patterson. Judgment was given by him on 30th June 1997 in which he refused to make the orders sought, on the grounds that this Tribunal was not a "Court or Tribunal" within the meaning of the Evidence (Proceedings in Other Jurisdictions) Act 1975 as applied to the Cayman Islands. The Tribunal has lodged a notice of appeal against this decision.

Taking of Evidence

The Tribunal first sat to hear evidence on 21st April 1997 and heard evidence from 21st April to 25th April inclusive and 28th April from the witnesses set out in Part I of the Sixth Schedule to this report.

On 25th April in the course of evidence being given by Mr. Noel Smyth, Solicitor to Mr. Ben Dunne, a legal question was raised as to the admissibility of certain evidence proposed to be given by Mr. Noel Smyth. This evidence related to conversations between Mr. Noel Smyth and Mr. Charles Haughey which Mr. Noel Smyth considered might be inadmissible due to the confidential nature of the conversations. Mr. Smyth had set out the contents of these conversations in a statement, but because of the possible inadmissibility in evidence of the conversations he was reluctant to show the statement to the Tribunal. The Tribunal decided that in the circumstances natural justice required that Mr. Charles Haughey be given an opportunity to see the statement and to make to the Tribunal such arguments as he wished with regard to the admissibility as evidence before the Tribunal of the facts set out therein. Accordingly, on the same day, the statement was delivered to Mr. Charles Haughey, unopened by the Tribunal, and he was invited to attend before the Tribunal either personally or by Counsel on 28th April. When the Tribunal resumed on that day Counsel for Mr. Charles Haughey sought and was granted representation before the Tribunal, limited, at his own request, to dealing with the issue of the admissibility of Mr. Noel Smyth's evidence. He requested an adjournment to consider the legal position, prepare submissions and advise his client. At this stage, in any event, the Tribunal required further time to allow the letters of request to be pursued, and to make further investigations arising out of some of the evidence given, and accordingly the Tribunal adjourned.

As a result of the evidence taken in London and the investigations made by the Tribunal, a considerable amount of information and documentation had become available to the Tribunal concerning, in particular, the alleged payments to Mr. Charles Haughey. Copies of all available statements and documentation not already furnished to Mr. Charles Haughey were furnished to him in mid-June 1997 and the Tribunal resumed its sittings on Monday 30th June.

At this sitting, Counsel on behalf of Mr. Charles Haughey sought and was granted full representation before the Tribunal in respect of all matters affecting Mr. Charles Haughey. He also stated that it was the intention of his client to furnish documents to the Tribunal by Friday 4th July dealing with all matters before the Tribunal concerning his client and he stated that these documents would acknowledge the evidence that, as a matter of probability, £1.3 million was paid into accounts managed by Mr. Desmond Traynor on behalf of Mr. Charles Haughey. Counsel for Mr. Charles Haughey also stated that the documents would make it clear that his client was not aware that Mr. Ben Dunne had transferred £1.1 million to Mr. Desmond Traynor intended for Mr. Charles Haughey's benefit, and would clarify that it was not the case that Mr. Charles Haughey personally received three bank drafts made payable to fictitious persons from Mr. Ben Dunne. Counsel for Mr. Charles Haughey then sought an adjournment for one week of the issue in relation to Mr. Noel Smyth's evidence. In view of the volume of documentation which had been furnished to Mr. Charles Haughey, the Tribunal considered it reasonable to grant such an adjournment.

The Tribunal sat again on 2nd July, 3rd July and 4th July to hear evidence, unconnected with Mr. Haughey.

No documents were in fact furnished to the Tribunal by Mr. Charles Haughey, but a statement was furnished by him to the Tribunal a few minutes before it sat on Monday 7th July. When the Tribunal sat Counsel for the Tribunal requested an adjournment for twenty four hours to consider the contents of the statement. Counsel for Mr. Charles Haughey then stated that he was not going to make any argument in relation to the issue of the confidentiality of the conversations between Mr. Noel Smyth and Mr. Charles Haughey, and accordingly Mr. Noel Smyth's statement in regard to these conversations was given to the Tribunal. The Tribunal then adjourned until the following day, 8th July.

While the Tribunal does not consider it appropriate as a general rule to publish statements made to it by potential witnesses, nevertheless, in the light of future events, the contents of Mr. Charles Haughey's statement of 7th July became very relevant. A copy of the statement is set out in the Seventh Schedule to this report.

On Tuesday 8th July Mr. Noel Smyth furnished information and a further document to the Tribunal. A copy of the document was furnished by the Tribunal to Counsel for Mr. Charles Haughey and the information was communicated to him. After considering these matters, Mr. Charles Haughey's Counsel requested an adjournment for a further 24 hours to allow him to consider the position, and this was granted.

The Tribunal then made an order for discovery by consent against Mr. Noel Smyth, and later on the same day he furnished an affidavit of discovery together with the documents referred to therein. He also furnished a further statement. Copies of these documents and the statement were immediately sent to the solicitors for Mr. Charles Haughey.

When the Tribunal sat on Wednesday 9th July Counsel for Mr. Charles Haughey said that he wished to read a statement by his client. In this statement Mr. Charles Haughey accepted that he received the £1.3 million from Mr. Ben Dunne, and stated that he became aware in 1993 that Mr. Ben Dunne was the donor. He furthermore accepted Mr. Ben Dunne's evidence that he had handed Mr. Haughey £210,000 in November 1991. He also said that until the previous day he had "mistakenly instructed my legal team". The Eighth Schedule to this report sets out the full text of this statement. When he came to give evidence on 15th July 1997 Mr. Charles Haughey read out a further statement the text of which is set out in the Ninth Schedule hereto. This report will comment more fully on these matters later.

The Tribunal then proceeded to hear evidence on 9th July, 10th July, 11th July, 14th July and 15th July. The witnesses who gave evidence on these days together with the witnesses who gave evidence on the 2nd, 3rd and 4th July 1997 are set out in Part II of the Sixth Schedule to this report. Oral submissions were taken by the Tribunal on 21st July.

Payments Made

From the evidence given and documents produced, the Tribunal is satisfied that a number of payments were made by the relevant parties which come within the terms of reference. These payments can be classified under a number of headings as follows:—

1. Ordinary political donations

2. Presidential Election

3. Waterworld plc

4. Fine Gael

5. Mr. Michael Lowry

6. Mr. Charles Haughey

7. Mr. Ciaran Haughey and Celtic Helicopters Ltd

It is proposed to deal with each of these classes separately in this report.

Chapter 4

Political Payments

Ordinary Political Donations

The Tribunal has had evidence of a number of contributions made, with one exception, by Mr. Ben Dunne personally, to various politicians and political organisations during the period in question. These are:—

(a) **Mr. Colm Hilliard**. The sum of £1,000 was given to him as a contribution to a Fianna Fáil fund raising event in November 1994, the proceeds of which were paid to the Fianna Fáil Ard Cumann.

(b) **Fianna Fáil Dublin South West Dáil Comhairle Cheantair**. The sum of £6,000 was contributed to the constituency organisation by Mr. Ben Dunne in March 1987.

(c) **Mr. Jim Mitchell**. The sum of £5,000 was contributed to him personally by way of cheque on 14th June 1988 by Mr. Ben Dunne with a request that the proceeds be divided between Mr. Jim Mitchell and Mr. John Bruton. Mr. Jim Mitchell complied with this request and retained £2,500.

(d) **Mr. John Bruton**. The sum of £2,500 was contributed by Mr. Ben Dunne on 14th June 1988 through Mr. Jim Mitchell.

(e) **The Limerick East Organisation of Fine Gael**. The sum of £2,000 was contributed by Mr. Ben Dunne in 1993 and the sum of £1,000 in 1994.

(f) **Mr. Michael Noonan**. The sum of £3,000 was contributed to him personally by Mr. Ben Dunne in 1992.

(g) **Mr. Ivan Yates**. The sum of £5,000 was contributed to him personally by Mr. Ben Dunne in November 1992.

(h) **Mr. Sean Barrett**. The sum of £1,000 was contributed to him personally by Mr. Ben Dunne in February 1987.

(i) **Mr. Fintan Coogan**. The sum of £5,000 was contributed to him personally by Mr. Ben Dunne in 1989.

(j) **The Wexford Branch of the Labour Party**. The sum of £100 was contributed through the local Dunnes Stores some time between 1990 and 1994.

(k) **Mr. Sean Haughey**. The sum of £1,000 was contributed to him personally by Mr. Ben Dunne in 1987 and a further sum of £1,000 in 1989.

(l) **Mr. Charles Haughey**. A cheque for £20,000 was given by Mr. Ben
Dunne to Mrs. Maureen Haughey on 14th June 1989 as a contribution
to the election campaign of Mr. Charles Haughey.

(m) **Mr. Michael Lowry**. The sum of £5,000 was contributed to him personally in 1992 by Mr. Ben Dunne.

The Tribunal is satisfied that all of these payments were normal political contributions, and, other than that to the Wexford Branch of the Labour Party,
were made by Mr. Ben Dunne on the basis of his personal regard for the
individuals or organisations concerned, and were amounts which he would
have considered to be relatively small. The Tribunal does not believe there
was any further motive behind those payments. The payment made to the
Wexford branch of the Labour Party was so small as to be insignificant.

Presidential Election

In the run up to the Presidential election in October 1990, Mr. Ben Dunne
was in the Barge Public House in Portobello, Dublin having a social drink
with a friend. On that evening there was a fund raising event in the Public
House organised by the Rathgar Branch of the Labour Party to raise funds
to support Mrs Mary Robinson's presidential campaign. Mr.Ruairi Quinn TD
was on the premises in connection with this function and approached Mr. Ben
Dunne and his friend, who was known to Mr.Ruairi Quinn. In the course of
the conversation which followed Mr.Ruairi Quinn told them why he was there,
and the conversation turned to funding the campaign of Mrs Mary Robinson.
At this stage, Mr. Ben Dunne went outside to his car, and came back with his
cheque book and wrote out a cheque for £15,000 in favour of the Labour
Party. The cheque was drawn on Mr. Ben Dunne's personal account and the
Tribunal is satisfied that it was a spontaneous gesture on the part of Mr. Ben
Dunne to contribute to Mrs Mary Robinson's campaign. The Tribunal is also
satisfied that the money was given by Mr. Ruairi Quinn to Mr. Ray Kavanagh,
the General Secretary of the Labour Party and was duly lodged in an account
to assist Mrs. Mary Robinson's campaign. While the cheque was made out in
favour of the Labour Party, the Tribunal is satisfied that in fact the motive in
making the payment was not to assist the Labour Party, but was to assist Mrs.
Mary Robinson personally in her campaign.

Waterworld plc

In early 1993 there was a project underway in the town of Tralee, Co.
Kerry to build an aquadome, which would act both as a facility for the local
community and as a tourist attraction. The project was organised on a local
community basis, and a company was formed to undertake this project. The

company was a non-profit making company limited by guarantee, and it was hoped that through the company local business could contribute to the development and become members of the company.

As Tralee was in the constituency of Mr. Dick Spring TD, the leader of the Labour Party, he was approached to assist in the fund raising for the project, which he agreed to do. He was aware that Dunnes Stores had recently opened a new store in the town of Tralee and he telephoned Mr. Ben Dunne in April 1993 asking for a contribution, on the basis that Dunnes Stores was carrying on business in the town. After a short discussion it was agreed that Mr. Ben Dunne would contribute £50,000, and a few days later he furnished to Mr. Dick Spring a cheque for this sum made out to Waterworld. The cheque was drawn on a Dunnes Stores Ireland Company account with the Ulster Bank and was duly received by Waterworld plc. and lodged to their account.

The Tribunal is quite satisfied that this was a normal transaction whereby Dunnes Stores were, for commercial reasons, prepared to contribute to a facility in a town in which they did business. The Tribunal is also satisfied that the payment conferred no benefit on either Mr. Dick Spring or on the Labour Party, nor was it intended to do so.

The Fine Gael Party

There were three occasions on which very substantial contributions were made by Mr. Ben Dunne to the Fine Gael Party. The circumstances in each case were as follows:

1. In 1989 Mr. Alan Dukes TD wrote to a large number of businesses and prominent businessmen seeking financial support for the Fine Gael Party. Mr. Ben Dunne was among the persons so contacted. Shortly after the letter was sent, a mutual friend suggested to Mr. Alan Dukes that he should personally contact Mr. Ben Dunne, which Mr. Alan Dukes duly did. A telephone conversation between them took place, in which Mr. Alan Dukes explained the purpose of the call, and Mr. Ben Dunne suggested that they should have dinner together. Arrangements were made, and ultimately Mr. and Mrs. Ben Dunne and Mr. and Mrs. Alan Dukes met on 13th October 1989 at Barberstown Castle. During the dinner Mr. Alan Dukes discussed Fine Gael policy, and in particular their position while in opposition, and sought a contribution to the party funds. After Mr. Ben Dunne had agreed in principle to make such a contribution, the sum of £30,000 was suggested by Mr. Alan Dukes. Mr. Ben Dunne agreed to give a cheque for that sum, and also suggested that he would make a similar contribution in each of the next two years. Towards the end of the evening Mr. Ben Dunne gave Mr. Alan Dukes a cheque for £30,000 drawn on an account in the Marino Dublin branch of the Bank of Ireland. This account was in the name of "Ben Dunne t/a 'Dunnes Stores' ", but was operated solely by Mr. Ben Dunne. This was one of

the accounts investigated by Price Waterhouse and Judge Buchanan. The further two annual payments of £30,000 each which it was suggested would be contributed were not in fact made by Mr. Ben Dunne.

2. In the early part of 1991, when Mr. John Bruton TD was Chairman of Fine Gael, the Party was facing serious financial difficulties. Mr. Michael Lowry was one of the chief fund-raisers for the Fine Gael Party at that time, and he suggested to Mr. John Bruton that an approach should be made to Mr. Ben Dunne for funds. Mr. John Bruton has said in evidence that he was in fact unaware of the earlier contribution of £30,000 by Mr. Ben Dunne. Mr. Michael Lowry and Mr. Ben Dunne had a close commercial relationship, as will be clear from a later portion of this report.

   A meeting between Mr. John Bruton and Mr. Ben Dunne was arranged for the evening of 24th April 1991 at Mr. Ben Dunne's home in Castleknock. Mr. Michael Lowry was present for some of the time at the meeting. It appears to have been a relatively short meeting over a cup of tea, in the course of which Mr. Ben Dunne gave Mr. John Bruton a cheque for £50,000 made out to Fine Gael and drawn on the same account in the Marino Dublin branch of the Bank of Ireland.

3. In May 1993 Mr. Ben Dunne gave a cheque for £100,000 to Mr. Ivan Doherty, who was then the General Secretary of Fine Gael, possibly through Mr. Michael Lowry. Mr. Ivan Doherty lodged this cheque to a bank account of a company which he controlled, and wrote a cheque on that account which was paid to Fine Gael. This money was lodged to Fine Gael's current account in the Bank of Ireland on 14th May 1993.

   Mr. Ivan Doherty had been told by Mr. Ben Dunne that he wanted to keep this payment confidential, and accordingly it was treated in this way to ensure that it would not appear in the name of Mr. Ben Dunne in the records of Fine Gael.

The evidence, particularly of Mrs. Margaret Heffernan, is that none of these payments were made with the authority or even with the knowledge of Dunnes Holding Company or of any of the Dunnes Stores Group companies, or indeed with the authority or with the knowledge of Mrs. Margaret Heffernan or of any of the other Directors of Dunnes Holding Company. It is, also, equally clear that the payments were made out of monies which were the property of the Dunnes Stores Group. The relationship between Mr. Ben Dunne and the Dunnes Stores Group, and the extent of his actions without authority, and his possible motives for making these payments will be commented on further in this report.

Chapter 5

Mr. Michael Lowry / Streamline Enterprises / Garuda Limited

Origin of Relationship

Mr. Michael Lowry started employment with Butler Refrigeration Limited in Thurles, Co. Tipperary in 1971 as an apprentice refrigeration engineer. He ultimately became Sales Manager of that company, and through that position came into contact with Dunnes Stores. By 1987 Butler Refrigeration Limited was carrying out a substantial amount of work for Dunnes Stores in the design, layout, installation and maintenance of refrigeration equipment.

Mr. Michael Lowry had for some years been involved in politics and in 1979 became a member of North Tipperary County Council. In 1987 he was elected a TD for the North Tipperary constituency, and in 1993 became Chairman of the Fine Gael Parliamentary Party. On 15th December 1994 he was appointed Minister for Transport, Energy and Communications. After his election as a TD, Mr. Michael Lowry was not able to continue in his position as Sales Manager of Butler Refrigeration Limited due to the demands on him and he left that employment on 31st December 1987. In the following year he was contacted by Mr. Owen Molloy, who as a Senior Executive in Dunnes Stores was responsible for developing the business in Great Britain and Northern Ireland. At Mr. Owen Molloy's request, Mr. Michael Lowry carried out some refrigeration work on a consultancy basis for Dunnes Stores in new food stores in Northern Ireland and in England. Mr. Owen Molloy was impressed with the work being done by Mr. Michael Lowry, and he spoke to Mr. Ben Dunne and recommended Mr. Michael Lowry to him. At this time, the refrigeration costs of Dunnes Stores were rising considerably, and Mr. Ben Dunne contacted Mr. Michael Lowry and ultimately a meeting was arranged in January 1989.

At this meeting, Mr. Ben Dunne said he was removing the contract for maintaining and equipping the refrigeration units in all the Dunnes Stores from Butler Refrigeration Limited, and he offered Mr. Michael Lowry the first option on the contract. A further meeting was held a few days later and it was agreed that initially Mr. Michael Lowry would have a contract in respect of the stores in the Munster area only. Mr. Michael Irwin, who was at that time the Chief Accountant to the Dunnes Stores Group, was then brought into the meeting, and was instructed by Mr. Ben Dunne to give Mr. Michael Lowry whatever financial support he needed to establish the business. No other financial arrangements appear to have been put in place at this stage. A short time afterwards, and the exact time is not clear from the evidence, Mr. Michael Lowry was offered the contract for the supply and maintenance of refrigeration units in all the Dunnes Stores in the Republic of Ireland.

In the meantime, on 11th August 1988, Mr. Michael Lowry incorporated a company called Garuda Limited, which traded under the name of Streamline Enterprises, and which will be referred to throughout this report as Streamline Enterprises. While the initial discussions regarding the contract for the Munster area appears to have been conducted very much on a personal basis with Mr. Michael Lowry, nevertheless Streamline Enterprises had in fact undertaken some of the work being done by Mr. Michael Lowry in the United Kingdom, and it was clear that this was the vehicle which was to be used by Mr. Michael Lowry for his business.

When the decision was taken to extend the contract to the entire of the Republic of Ireland, further discussions took place at which the financial position of both Streamline Enterprises and Mr. Michael Lowry were discussed. In February 1989 Streamline Enterprises prepared costings for the work. It is clear that once the overall contract was agreed, Streamline Enterprises existed for one purpose only, namely to perform the contract with Dunnes Stores Group. The arrangement reached was that the Dunnes Stores auditors, Oliver Freaney & Company, were to be appointed auditors of Streamline Enterprises, and Mr. Michael Irwin, Chief Accountant to the Dunnes Stores Group, was to have full access to the books and records of Streamline Enterprises. Dunnes Stores Group were to supply, and did supply, initial capital to enable the business to start up. In effect, Streamline Enterprises became a business with only one customer and its future was totally linked to retaining the goodwill of Dunnes Stores. In fact it was virtually subsumed into the Dunnes Stores Group and was regarded by them, and probably by Mr. Michael Lowry, as being in effect a division of the Dunnes Stores Group.

In the discussions relating to the final contract, which took place between Mr. Ben Dunne, Mr. Michael Lowry and Mr. Michael Irwin, it was agreed that Streamline Enterprises would make a small profit, which Mr. Michael Irwin says was envisaged at between £20,000 and £50,000 per annum, but in addition, in the words of Mr. Michael Irwin, "on a second level, Mr. Lowry for his product management skills, so to speak, was going to get a bonus separately from Mr. Dunne." Mr. Michael Lowry accepts that Mr. Ben Dunne gave him an assurance in the following words, namely:—

> "The bottom line is, if you are good for Dunnes Stores and if you achieve the savings that I think are possible, I will certainly make it worth your while and your company will be successful and you will be a wealthy man."

No further financial details were agreed, and there appears to have been no discussion as to the basis on which the company would charge the Dunnes Stores Group, and thereby make the profit. Neither was there any discussion as to the amount or the method of the payments to be made to Mr. Michael

Lowry personally. Mr. Michael Lowry apparently had such faith in the generosity of Mr. Ben Dunne that he agreed to these terms.

In accordance with the agreement, Dunnes Stores financed the start-up costs of Streamline Enterprises, including the cost of acquiring a site and constructing a warehouse at Abbey Road in Thurles. It was originally intended that the site and warehouse would be owned by Mr. Michael Lowry and his wife through a company called Green Holdings Limited, but ultimately the land was taken in the name of Garuda Limited. In all, Dunnes Stores appeared to have paid £165,000 to Streamline Enterprises in relation to this warehouse. These payments were treated in the books of both Dunnes Stores and Streamline Enterprises as being a loan which, at least according to the records of both companies, was paid off over a period of some four years. However, this appears to have been primarily a book-keeping exercise, as the books of both companies were kept by the auditors of Dunnes Stores, namely Oliver Freaney & Company. In Mr. Michael Irwin's words, the loan was repaid "by allowing Streamline to make a certain amount of profit and off-set it against the loan which they owed us." In Mr. Michael Lowry's words "they would be giving me sufficient margins to ensure I could meet my liabilities in respect of that". As Dunnes Stores decided how much profit they would "allow" Streamline Enterprises to make, it could be said that in a sense this whole transaction was a sham, and that in fact Dunnes Stores simply contributed some £165,000 to Streamline Enterprises in the same way as they would have contributed it to a division of their own company. This whole transaction reflects the nature of the relationship between Dunnes Stores and Streamline Enterprises, and the amount of control exercised by Dunnes Stores.

Payments to Mr. Michael Lowry Personally

The business relationship between Streamline Enterprises and Dunnes Stores prospered. Streamline Enterprises provided an efficient and cost effective service and undoubtedly brought about substantial savings for Dunnes Stores. Between 1989 and the end of 1996 the turnover of Streamline Enterprises, which was solely in relation to Dunnes Stores, was in excess of £12m. The Tribunal is not concerned with the payments made to Streamline Enterprises in the normal course of business, save to say that Streamline Enterprises made a modest profit as had been agreed. However, during this period a number of payments were made by Mr. Ben Dunne personally, or on his instructions, which were clearly outside normal business relations. Five of these payments were identified in Judge Buchanan's report, all of which were made from the Dunnes Stores account at the Marino Dublin branch of the Bank of Ireland. These payments were as follows:

1. A cheque for £6,000 dated 20th December 1989 payable to Mr. Michael Lowry. This cheque was cashed by Mr. Michael Lowry.

2. A cheque for £8,500 dated 21st December 1990 payable to cash. This cheque was paid into Mr. Michael Lowry's personal account in the Thurles, Co. Tipperary branch of the Bank of Ireland.

3. A cheque for £6,500 dated 10th July 1991 payable to M. Lowry. This cheque was paid into the personal account of Mr. Michael Lowry at the Dame Street Dublin branch of Allied Irish Banks.

4. A cheque for £8,000 dated 11th December 1991 payable to cash. This cheque was also lodged in the personal account of Mr. Michael Lowry in the Dame Street Dublin branch of Allied Irish Bank.

5. A cheque for £12,000 dated 15th December 1992 payable to cash. This cheque was cashed by Mr. Michael Lowry.

All these cheques were drawn on the account at the Marino Dublin branch of the Bank of Ireland, and were signed by Mr. Michael Irwin. In each case the cheques were issued by Mr. Michael Irwin on the instructions of Mr. Ben Dunne. A curious feature of this account is that Mrs. Margaret Heffernan's evidence is that this account was operated solely by Mr. Ben Dunne, and that neither she nor her fellow directors knew anything about it. However, both she and Mr. Ben Dunne acknowledge that the monies in the account were the property of Dunnes Stores, and Mr. Ben Dunne maintains that there was no particular significance in the payments being made out of that account. While that may be so, the fact that the account existed and the payments were made out of it without the knowledge of the board of the company shows the extent of the financial control which Mr. Ben Dunne had over the affairs of Dunnes Stores at the relevant time. It would appear that he was able to issue cheques at will, or direct Mr. Michael Irwin to do so, without authority from anybody else, and frequently did so. It is certainly strange that the financial affairs of one of the country's largest commercial enterprises should be controlled solely by one man.

These payments, with the exception of the £6,500 payment, were made on the instructions of Mr. Ben Dunne for the purpose of paying Christmas bonuses to the staff of Streamline Enterprises. The £6,500 payment is believed by Mr. Michael Lowry to have been the reimbursement of expenses incurred by Streamline Enterprises in the storage facility which had been erected by Dunnes Stores, but the cheque does not appear to have been paid into an account of Streamline Enterprises, but rather into Mr. Michael Lowry's personal account at the Dame Street Dublin branch of Allied Irish Banks. Mr. Michael Lowry's evidence is that the other payments were in fact used for paying staff bonuses, and from such enquiries as the Tribunal have been able to make, it is clear that bonuses were paid, although it has not been possible to confirm that all the monies were used for this purpose.

Cheques to Streamline Enterprises

Between November 1988 and March 1993 there were a number of cheques issued by the Dunnes Stores Group in favour of Streamline Enterprises which were in fact either cashed by Mr. Michael Lowry or lodged by him to his own account. These cheques are listed in the Tenth Schedule hereto. Mr. Michael Lowry's evidence is that these were payments for work carried out by him either in England or Northern Ireland as a Consultant to Dunnes Stores, or for equipment supplied by him to Dunnes Stores. The first payment on 14th November 1988 was in Irish currency while the other payments were in sterling.

The payment of £6,000 in Irish currency on the 14th November 1988 was lodged by Mr. Michael Lowry to his personal account in the Bank of Ireland in Thurles, Co. Tipperary. The next six payments, between 13th December 1988 and 14th September 1990, and varying between £5,000 sterling and £19,730 sterling, were cashed by Mr. Michael Lowry.

The payment of £34,100 sterling on 3rd September 1991 was lodged by Mr. Michael Lowry to an account which he held in a subsidiary branch of Allied Irish Bank in the Channel Islands. This account was in the name of Mr. Michael Lowry and his three children, and appears to have been opened on the 3rd September 1991 by a deposit of £100,000 sterling, which presumably included the sum of £34,100 sterling.

Finally, the payment on 15th March 1993 of £55,314 sterling was lodged by Mr. Michael Lowry to his personal account at the Dame Street Dublin branch of Allied Irish Banks.

The Tribunal cannot accept Mr. Michael Lowry's evidence that these monies were paid by Dunnes Stores to him personally for work carried out by him personally. All these payments were made by Dunnes Stores in respect of work invoiced to them in the name of Streamline Enterprises, the cheques were made payable to Streamline Enterprises, and all paperwork in connection with the payments were in the name of Streamline Enterprises. In spite of this, it appears from Mr. Michael Lowry's evidence that these transactions were not reflected in the accounts of Streamline Enterprises. Mr. Michael Lowry's explanation is that the payments would not appear in the books of the company *"because I had already declared it as personal income to myself"*.

The Tribunal is satisfied that as far as Dunnes Stores were concerned these payments were being made to Streamline Enterprises for work carried out by that firm. Neither Mr. Ben Dunne nor Mr. Michael Irwin ever suggested in their evidence in relation to the relationship between Dunnes Stores and Mr. Michael Lowry that there was a personal consultancy arrangement between Mr. Michael Lowry and Dunnes Stores. They merely stated that Mr. Michael Lowry would personally be paid a bonus. Signficantly, when they were cross examined on behalf of Mr. Michael Lowry, it was never suggested to either of them that there was such a consultancy arrangement. The Tribunal is quite satisfied that no such arrangement existed and that Dunnes Stores at all times intended these payments to be made to Streamline Enterprises, and not to Mr. Michael Lowry personally.

Bonus Payments to Mr. Michael Lowry

In addition to these sums, there were several substantial payments made by Mr. Ben Dunne to Mr. Michael Lowry personally. These were as follows:

1. The sum of £25,000 sterling was paid to Mr. Michael Lowry on 9th October 1990. This payment was made by three cheques, each for £8,181.00 sterling and one cheque for £457.00 sterling. These cheques were again drawn on the account with the Marino Dublin branch of the Bank of Ireland. Mr. Ben Dunne has told the Tribunal that he made this payment, but cannot recollect why it was made in this manner. The cheques were lodged by Mr. Michael Lowry to an account in his name in Bank of Ireland (I.O.M.) Limited in the Isle of Man. Mr. Michael Lowry's evidence is that this account was opened on the instigation of Mr. Ben Dunne. While this may well be so, Mr. Michael Lowry allowed the monies to remain in that account until 20th May 1992 when he transferred it to an account which he held in the Patrick Street Cork branch of the Irish Permanent Building Society.

2. The sum of £40,000 sterling was on 1st August 1991 transferred on the instructions of Mr. Ben Dunne from an account in the name of Tutbury Limited, an Isle of Man company controlled by Mr. Ben Dunne, in Rea Brothers (Isle of Man) Limited, an Isle of Man bank, to a newly opened account in the same bank in the name of Badgeworth Limited, another Isle of Man company. This money remained on deposit in the account of Badgeworth Limited until 5th May 1992 when the account was closed and a bank draft for £42,567.26 sterling was issued by Rea Brothers (Isle of Man) Limited payable to Mr. Michael Lowry. On 18th May 1992 the proceeds of this bank draft were paid into the account of Michael Lowry at the Patrick Street, Cork branch of the Irish Permanent Building Society.

3. The sum of £40,000 was paid to Mr. Michael Lowry by way of a bank draft drawn on the Bank of Ireland on the instructions of Rea Brothers (Isle of Man) Limited, which draft was paid for out of the account of Tutbury Limited in that bank on 29th May 1992. The proceeds of this draft were paid into Mr. Michael Lowry's account at the Patrick Street, Cork branch of the Irish Permanent Building Society.

4. The sum of £50,000 was paid by Mr. Ben Dunne to Mr. Michael Lowry on 27th May 1992 by way of a cheque made payable to Streamline Enterprises and drawn on the number seven account of Dunnes Stores Ireland Company with the College Green Dublin branch of Ulster Bank Limited. This cheque was endorsed on the back by Mr. Michael Lowry on behalf of Streamline Enterprises, and was lodged by him to

his said account in the Patrick Street, Cork branch of the Irish Permanent Building Society.

Tutbury Limited was a company incorporated in the Isle of Man which was controlled by Mr. Ben Dunne. The funds in the account were the property of Dunnes Stores and originated from profits made by companies associated with Dunnes Stores in the Far East. The account appears to have been under the sole control of Mr. Ben Dunne although many of the transactions appear to have been carried out by Mr. Ben Dunne's solicitor, Mr. Noel Smyth, on Mr. Ben Dunne's instructions.

Badgeworth Limited was also a company incorporated in the Isle of Man. It was incorporated on the instructions of Mr. Noel Smyth, whose evidence is that he did so on the instructions of Mr. Ben Dunne. The latter confirms that the company was set up by Mr. Noel Smyth for Mr. Michael Lowry on Mr. Ben Dunne's instructions. It is clear that while Mr. Michael Lowry did not give instructions for the incorporation of Badgeworth Limited, nor that an account in the Isle of Man be opened in the name of that company, he was aware that the payment was being made for his benefit in this way, and he allowed the money to remain in that account until he had need of it in Ireland.

Work to Mr. Michael Lowry's House

In 1992 Mr. Michael Lowry purchased a house at Holy Cross, Co. Tipperary which was in need of refurbishment. Around the same time, and probably because of this purchase, he spoke to Mr. Michael Irwin about trying to reconcile the financial situation as between Streamline Enterprises and Dunnes Stores. He approached Mr. Ben Dunne and told him of the purchase and his need for funds to refurbish and extend the house, and Mr. Ben Dunne agreed that Dunnes Stores would assist him financially. It appears that Mr. Ben Dunne had in his own mind a figure of £200,000 as the probable cost, but it is not clear whether the actual figure was every discussed with Mr. Michael Lowry. Mr. Michael Lowry also discussed the position with Mr. Michael Irwin and asked him to recommend an architect and contractor. Mr. Michael Irwin told him that a contractor called Faxhill Homes Limited and an architect called Mr. Peter Stevens were already carrying out work for Dunnes Stores, and had carried out work on Mr. Ben Dunne's house. He recommended that Mr. Michael Lowry should instruct them to carry out the required works.

The first contact with Mr. Peter Stevens appears to have been made by Mr. Ben Dunne who asked him to meet Mr. Michael Lowry and find out his requirements. It is quite clear that both Mr. Peter Stevens and Faxhill Homes Limited were being instructed by Dunnes Stores and/or Mr. Ben Dunne rather than by Mr. Michael Lowry. Mr. Peter Stevens drew up plans in consultation with Mr. Michael Lowry and his wife, and had a number of subsequent meetings with Mr. Michael Lowry, but only in connection with the actual work to be done. Mr. Peter Stevens had a preliminary costing done by a quantity surveyor, who estimated the cost at just over £216,000. However, as the work progressed, the cost turned out to be a great deal more. In all, Dunnes Stores paid the contractors £395,107 for the work which was carried out.

Payment was made to the contractor on foot of certificates issued by Mr. Peter Stevens. These certificates were issued to Dunnes Stores and the payments were made by Dunnes Stores on foot of them. While a dispute exists between Dunnes Stores and Mr. Michael Lowry as to the actual value of the work carried out, there is no doubt that Dunnes Stores paid Faxhill Homes Limited £395,107 on foot of certificates for that amount issued by Mr. Peter Stevens.

In the books of Dunnes Stores Group the payments for the work on Mr. Michael Lowry's house were treated as having being payments for work done for Dunnes Stores at the Ilac Centre in Dublin.

This was queried by Mr. Michael Irwin, but Mr. Ben Dunne insisted that this was the procedure which ought to be followed. It is significant that Mr. Michael Irwin, as the company's accountant, felt that this was a very inefficient way of treating the payments from Dunnes Stores point of view, and that if it had been treated as a payment to Streamline Enterprises and/or Mr. Michael Lowry for work done by them, it would have been tax deductible by Dunnes Stores. It is also significant that the method of payment used ensured that there was no record of these payments being made for the benefit of Mr. Michael Lowry, and this seems to have been the clear intention of Mr. Ben Dunne when he insisted that the payment be made in this way.

Statement to Dáil Éireann

On 19ᵗʰ December 1996 Mr. Michael Lowry made a personal statement to Dáil Éireann. It purported to "set the record straight" and to cover, inter alia, his relationship with Dunnes Stores. In the course of the statement Mr. Michael Lowry maintained that the money spent on his house was not a loan, nor a gift, nor a hand-out, but was income, being payment on account for professional services to Dunnes Stores. He also maintained that it was never intended to be a tax evasion measure by him. He then went on to state:—

> "Having been publicly criticised to an unprecedented level I ask your patience and indulgence to enable me to take you through the sequence of events which led to the formation of my company, its legitimate commercial operations, the outline of services provided, the financial arrangements and method of payment and to the fact that despite all my efforts, I have unfinished business with Dunnes Stores and, therefore, with the Revenue Commissioners".

In dealing with his initial arrangements with Dunnes Stores, he commented:—

> "Mr. Dunne said that I should leave it to his judgement to make a decision on profits but clearly stated that he would put the company in profit and also remunerate me separately for my technical advice and

for the project management of the various jobs. There was also to be a performance bonus."

He then referred to having become aware of the Price Waterhouse Report, although he had not actually seen it. He said:—

"However, I understand, after numerous enquiries, that apart from the house transactions there are two other references to my business in that report. The payment of £50,000 was income payable to me under my arrangement with Dunnes Stores, on which tax has been paid. The sums of £6,000 and £6,500 were paid as bonuses by Dunnes Stores for the staff of Streamline Enterprises, not including me. Those payments were made in cash, without deduction of tax."

This is the only reference in his statement to sums of money having been paid to him personally, and in fact Mr. Michael Lowry now maintains that the sum of £6,500 was not paid as a bonus, but was to reimburse him for monies spent on the storage facility in Thurles, Co. Tipperary. Mr. Michael Lowry in his statement makes no mention whatever of the other large payments of £25,000 sterling, £40,000 sterling and £40,000 respectively, nor does he mention the other sums which were paid to him to be used as bonuses.

The final passage from Mr. Michael Lowry's statement which calls for comment is that he stated:—

"I did not make any secret of the fact that Dunnes Stores paid me for professional services by way of assistance towards my house. If someone were trying to hide income, would he or she not be more likely to put it in an off-shore account? The last thing such a person would do would be to spend it on a very obvious structure of bricks and mortar for all the world to see."

In the light of the fact that Mr. Michael Lowry had had two off-shore accounts in his own name, one in the Bank of Ireland in the Isle of Man and the other in an Allied Irish Banks subsidiary in Jersey, and had held money in an Isle of Man account in the name of Badgeworth Limited, this part of his statement must be viewed with some astonishment. Mr. Michael Lowry's Counsel strongly urged that it is not for this Tribunal to determine whether Mr. Michael Lowry deliberately misled the Dáil, and the Tribunal accepts, that on the authorities quoted by him, this is a matter for the Dáil itself. However, the Tribunal is entitled to take into account his apparent lack of candour in assessing the motives behind the financial arrangements which he had with Dunnes Stores, and with Mr. Ben Dunne in particular.

Political Favours by Mr. Michael Lowry

The Tribunal has made extensive enquiries as to the possibility of political influence being used by Mr. Michael Lowry in favour of the Dunnes Stores Group or any of the shareholders thereof. Only two very minor incidents came to the notice of the Tribunal, and in fairness to Mr. Michael Lowry, brief mention should be made of them.

Firstly, evidence was given by Mr. Paul McGrath TD, who is a Fine Gael member of the Dáil for the Westmeath constituency, and is also a member of Westmeath County Council. There was a shopping centre development proposed in Mullingar, and Dunnes Stores was to be the anchor tenant. There was a proposal that the area in which the development was to take place should be designated as an urban renewal area for tax purposes, and this matter was discussed at Westmeath County Council. Mr. Paul McGrath was opposed to such designation, primarily as he felt this might give Dunnes Stores a commercial advantage over local small businesses, and he voted against the proposed designation. Shortly afterwards, he had a chance meeting with Mr. Michael Lowry in a corridor in Leinster House, and in the course of their conversation Mr. Michael Lowry indicated that he was aware of Mr. Paul McGrath's opposition to the designated status for this development, and he suggested that Mr. Paul McGrath should not continue his opposition. Mr. Paul McGrath also has given evidence that Mr. Michael Lowry based his request on the fact that Mr. Ben Dunne was a major contributor to the Fine Gael Party, although Mr. Michael Lowry does not recollect saying this.

The Tribunal is quite satisfied that this incident has no significance whatsoever. In fact, Mr. Michael Lowry was requested to intervene, not by Dunnes Stores, but by a representative on behalf of the developer. The conversation took place after the vote had been taken, and in any event the ultimate decision as to whether to give the area designated status was not a decision for the County Council, but was a government decision, which neither Mr. Michael Lowry nor Mr. Paul McGrath could have influenced in any way, as Fine Gael was in opposition at the time.

The second incident concerns a prosecution in the District Court in Cork of a Dunnes Stores company in respect of a consignment of potatoes on sale at their store in Ballyvolane. When the local store manager, Mr. Bernard Walsh, received the summons he decided to telephone Mr. Michael Lowry to ask what the procedure was. He was particularly concerned because the summons appeared to have been issued by the Minister for Agriculture rather than the Southern Health Board. Mr. Michael Lowry made some enquiries from Mr. Michael Miley, who was the Programme Manager for the Minister for Agriculture at the time, and having got some information from him, Mr. Michael Lowry then telephoned Mr. Bernard Walsh and told him that the summons was going to be adjourned, and was being dealt with by the State Solicitors Office in Cork.

The Tribunal is quite satisfied that there was nothing improper in what took place, and that the only reason that Mr. Bernard Walsh contacted Mr. Michael Lowry was that he was a personal friend.

The Tribunal concludes, therefore, that neither Dunnes Stores nor Mr. Ben Dunne ever requested Mr. Michael Lowry to make any personal or political intervention on their behalf, and equally the Tribunal is satisfied that Mr. Michael Lowry never sought to intervene in any way for the benefit of Dunnes

Stores or Mr. Ben Dunne. The Tribunal is satisfied that there was no political impropriety on the part of Mr. Michael Lowry.

Dunnes Stores / Mr. Michael Lowry Relationship

In his evidence, Mr. Ben Dunne explained that part of his business philosophy was that he thought bonus payments were an important way of encouraging people or of getting a better performance out of people. It is clear that the large sums of money paid to Mr. Michael Lowry personally, and the money expended on his house, were part of this philosophy. There is no doubt that, from the commercial point of view of Dunnes Stores, it was a successful policy in that Mr. Michael Lowry and Streamline Enterprises certainly performed their work for Dunnes Stores at a very high level. However, the method by which these bonuses were paid goes far beyond the business practice of rewarding extra work with extra benefits. The Tribunal is satisfied that the two bank accounts in the Isle of Man, one in the name of Mr. Michael Lowry and the other in the name of Badgeworth Limited, were set up at the instigation of Mr. Ben Dunne and not of Mr. Michael Lowry. This of course does not exonerate Mr. Michael Lowry, as he allowed the money to remain in these accounts until he had need of it in Ireland. In any event, Mr. Michael Lowry was quite happy to operate off-shore bank accounts, as is shown by the account which he held in the Allied Irish Banks subsidiary in Jersey.

The Tribunal is satisfied that the arrangement whereby Mr. Michael Lowry would be paid substantial sums of money on a personal basis, and ultimately have a large sum of money spent on renovations to his house, was designed to assist him in evading tax. The Tribunal is also satisfied that Mr. Ben Dunne knowingly assisted Mr. Michael Lowry in evading tax. This view would be confirmed by the fact that the first two substantial payments to Michael Lowry, of £25,000 and £40,000 respectively, were both in sterling and were both initially paid into bank accounts in the Isle of Man. There is further confirmation in the way in which the house refurbishment was dealt with, and in particular in the fact that the payments for this refurbishment did not appear in the books of Dunnes Stores as being payments either to Mr. Michael Lowry or to Streamline Enterprises. When this was suggested to Mr. Ben Dunne in evidence, his reaction was:—

> "Certainly when it came to Mr. Lowry as to tax, I would believe then and would believe now that Mr. Lowry is old enough and mature enough to be able to take care of his own tax problems, and I wouldn't have been involved in anything like that".

This is a completely naive and unacceptable explanation. Indeed, it is preceded by an acknowledgement by Mr. Ben Dunne that he might have arranged that people get small Christmas bonuses under the counter. The Tribunal is satisfied that these were very large bonuses, but still were being paid, in effect, under the counter.

The Tribunal is also satisfied that Mr. Michael Lowry's motive in accepting these payments personally, and in entering into the arrangement whereby he would be paid bonuses personally, was to enable him to evade tax. He operated his business on two levels, on one level through the company, which made a small profit and duly paid its taxes, and on a second level whereby large sums of money were paid to him personally in a clandestine manner. While the Tribunal accepts that Streamline Enterprises made large savings for the Dunnes Stores Group, it is unacceptable to make this a justification for Mr. Michael Lowry's behaviour. He has sought to argue that if normal commercial mark ups had been applied to the goods supplied to Dunnes Stores, this would have amounted to a considerably greater figure than the bonuses paid to him. This is a totally flawed argument, as if a normal commercial relationship had existed, the additional monies would have been paid to Streamline Enterprises and not to Mr. Michael Lowry personally, with all the taxation consequences which that would have entailed.

The relationship between Dunnes Stores and Mr. Michael Lowry and Streamline Enterprises was extraordinary. On the one hand, it allowed Dunnes Stores to have virtually complete control over the business of Streamline Enterprises, and on the other hand it allowed payments to be made to Mr. Michael Lowry in a completely unorthodox fashion which facilitated tax evasion. Putting it at its mildest, it was an unhealthy business relationship, leaving aside the political implications altogether. While there appears to have been no benefit to Dunnes Stores other than a commercial benefit from this relationship, the potential consequences of it are extremely disturbing in at least three aspects.

Firstly, by evading tax in this way, Mr. Michael Lowry made himself vulnerable to all kinds of pressures from Dunnes Stores, had they chosen to apply these pressures. The threat to disclose the payments and the off-shore accounts could have been used by Dunnes Stores to obtain favours, as indeed could a threat to cut off this source of income to Mr. Michael Lowry.

Secondly, quite apart from pressure from Dunnes Stores, should the existence of these accounts have become known to any third party, such third party could have sought either political or financial favours in return for silence. As has been seen, the disclosure of these matters has had a catastrophic effect on the personal and political life of Mr. Michael Lowry, and therefore the threat of disclosure would have been a powerful weapon in the hands of any third party, leaving Mr. Michael Lowry open to blackmail of various kinds.

Thirdly, and perhaps the most damaging aspect of this relationship, is that there could be a public perception that a person in the position of a Government Minister and member of Cabinet was able to ignore, and indeed cynically evade, both the taxation and exchange control laws of the State with impunity. Loss of revenue to the black economy is a serious matter for the State, and it is an appalling situation that a Government Minister and Chairman of a Parliamentary Party can be seen to have been consistently benefiting from the black economy from shortly after he was first elected to Dáil Éireann. If such a person can behave in this way without serious sanctions being imposed, it becomes very difficult to condemn others who similarly flout the law.

Chapter 6

Background to Payments to Mr. Charles Haughey

Introduction

The relationship between Mr. Ben Dunne and Mr. Charles Haughey was a strange and complex one. Mr. Charles Haughey has now admitted that he received five payments from Mr. Ben Dunne amounting in all to some £1.3 million. However, when asked at the early stages of the Tribunal of Inquiry whether he had received the benefit of any of these monies, Mr. Charles Haughey denied any knowledge of them and denied having obtained any benefit from them. As a result of this denial the Tribunal undertook extensive investigations to trace the monies paid by Mr. Ben Dunne, and also to find the sources of income of Mr. Charles Haughey. The result of these investigations was that the Tribunal became satisfied beyond all reasonable doubt that all of the monies paid by Mr. Ben Dunne were received by or on behalf of Mr. Charles Haughey for his benefit or, in one case, for the benefit of a member of his family. The Tribunal acknowledges that there are some missing links, in particular in relation to the regulating of accounts in Ansbacher Cayman Limited, a Cayman Islands bank, the machinery for debiting and crediting those accounts and the knowledge of Mr. Charles Haughey in relation thereto. The Tribunal believes that the only way in which these matters could be determined would be from information and documentation which is in the possession of either Ansbacher Cayman Limited or the representatives of its former joint managing director Mr. John Furze, who is now deceased.

This report will set out the Tribunal's knowledge to date and will try to explain the complicated transactions which took place. In order to understand these transactions, it is necessary to give a short account of the various persons involved, and the various banks involved.

Mr. Charles Haughey

Mr. Charles Haughey qualified as a Chartered Accountant in the 1940s and shortly afterwards set up in partnership with Mr. Harry Boland under the name Haughey Boland. He is also a qualified barrister-at-law. In the year 1966 he left the accountancy practice. He commenced a successful career in public life in 1957 when he was first elected to Dáil Éireann and remained a member continuously until June 1992.

33

He held the following offices in the course of his parliamentary career:—

1960 and 1961 Parliamentary Secretary

1961 — 1964 Minister for Justice

1964 — 1966 Minister for Agriculture

1966 — 1970 Minister for Finance

1977 — 1979 Minister for Health and Social Welfare

1979 — 1981 Taoiseach

1982   Taoiseach

1987 — 1989 Taoiseach

1989 — 1992 Taoiseach

In the early 1970s Mr. Charles Haughey purchased Abbeville, a large Gandon designed house with substantial lands in Kinsealy in North County Dublin. Over the years, particularly when he was not in office, he carried out farming activities on the lands. It would appear that he enjoyed a lavish lifestyle although he denied this in evidence, and there is no doubt that the upkeep of Abbeville must have required considerable funds.

Mr. Desmond Traynor

The late Mr. Desmond Traynor was a Chartered Accountant who started his career in Haughey Boland and was articled to Mr. Charles Haughey. He was a successful businessman and banker. On 11th December 1969 he was appointed a director of Guinness & Mahon (Ireland) Limited, which was a licensed bank and on 13th May 1976 he was appointed Deputy Chairman, which was a full time executive position under which he was de facto Chief Executive of the bank. He remained in that position until his resignation on 2nd May 1986. Shortly after his resignation he was appointed chairman of Cement Roadstone Holdings plc, which entitled him to an office at the headquarters of that company. He died on 11th May 1994.

In 1969 Guinness & Mahon (Ireland) Limited formed a small investment company in the Cayman Islands, which will be dealt with in detail later in this report. Mr. Desmond Traynor was responsible for setting up this company, which became a Class A licensed bank in late 1972. In 1974 he became chairman of the Cayman Bank and remained in this position until his death in 1994.

Mr. Noel Fox

Mr. Noel Fox is a Chartered Accountant and is a senior partner in the firm of Oliver Freaney & Company, and has been a partner in that firm since 1963. Oliver Freaney & Company are auditors of some of the companies in the Dunnes Stores Group. In addition, Mr. Noel Fox was a financial adviser to the Dunnes Stores Group, and in particular was a trusted adviser to and close personal friend of Mr. Ben Dunne. For some years he also attended daily early morning meetings of the Dunnes Stores Group. He has been one of the trustees of the Dunnes Settlement Trust since 1972, and in that capacity was one of the defendants in the action taken by Mr. Ben Dunne against the trustees.

Guinness & Mahon (Ireland) Limited

The firm of Guinness & Mahon was founded in 1836 by John Ross Mahon and Robert Rundell Guinness. It commenced business as a land agency but subsequently became a bank. In 1873 it established a sub-office in London and by 1923 the sub-office became in fact the headquarters of the bank. At this time the bank was known as Guinness Mahon & Co. In 1966 Guinness & Mahon Limited was formed as a subsidiary of the London company. On 31st August 1994 it was acquired by Irish Permanent plc and its name was changed to Guinness & Mahon (Ireland) Limited which will be the name used throughout this report to identify it. As already stated, Mr. Desmond Traynor was deputy chairman and de facto Chief Executive of Guinness & Mahon (Ireland) Limited from May 1976 to May 1986.

Mr. Padraig Collery

Mr. Padraig Collery joined Guinness & Mahon (Ireland) Limited as a senior bank official in 1974 having previously been a bank official with Lloyds Bank in London. His main area of responsibility in the bank was the management of the operations department, which was responsible for the maintenance of all the customer accounts of the bank. He was also responsible for the computer operations in the bank. He left Guinness & Mahon (Ireland) Limited in 1989, but appears to have retained close contacts with Mr. Desmond Traynor up to the time of Mr. Desmond Traynor's death.

Mr. John Furze

Mr. John Furze had worked in the Cayman Islands for some years with the Bank of Nova Scotia. When Guinness & Mahon (Ireland) Limited set up its Cayman Islands subsidiary, Guinness Mahon Cayman Trust Limited, that company was managed for Guinness & Mahon (Ireland) Limited by the Bank of Nova Scotia, and Mr. John Furze and Mr. John Collins were the officials responsible for its management. In 1973 Mr. John Furze and Mr. John Collins left the Bank of Nova Scotia and became full-time joint managing directors of Guinness Mahon Cayman Trust Limited. Over the years, Mr. John Furze maintained a very close relationship with Mr. Desmond Traynor. Mr. Desmond Traynor introduced a number of Irish customers to the Cayman Bank, and the affairs of these customers appear to have been looked after by

Mr. John Furze in conjunction with Mr. Desmond Traynor. It is noted with regret that Mr. John Furze died on 25th July 1997.

Mr. Paul Carty

Mr. Paul Carty is also a Chartered Accountant. He joined the firm of Haughey Boland as a senior audit assistant in February 1968, was made a partner in December 1971 and remained with that firm through various mergers. The firm now forms a part of the large accountancy practice known as Deloitte & Touche of which Mr. Paul Carty is currently the managing partner.

Mr. Jack Stakelum

Mr. Jack Stakelum is a Chartered Accountant who completed his articles with Haughey Boland, and was articled to Mr. Charles Haughey. After some time with another firm, he returned to Haughey Boland in 1962 and was made a partner in 1967. He left Haughey Boland in November 1975 and set up his own financial consultancy practice under the name Business Enterprises Limited. He was a close personal friend of Mr. Desmond Traynor.

Ansbacher Cayman Limited

Guinness & Mahon (Ireland) Limited set up a subsidiary company in the Cayman Islands in 1969 which was known as Guinness Mahon Cayman Trust Limited. It was originally managed by the Bank of Nova Scotia on behalf of Guinness & Mahon (Ireland) Limited but subsequently became a bank in its own right. Mr. John Furze and Mr. John Collins were joint managing directors until 1995, and Mr. John Collins still remains a non-executive director. In 1984 Guinness Mahon Cayman Trust Limited was sold by Guinness & Mahon (Ireland) Limited to Guinness Mahon & Co. Limited in London, its parent company, and the next year it was sold on to a consortium which included Mr. Desmond Traynor, Mr. John Furze and Mr. John Collins. They in turn sold a 75% interest to a London Bank called Henry Ansbacher & Co., a member of the Ansbacher Group, and the name of the bank was changed from Guinness Mahon Cayman Trust Limited to Ansbacher Limited. It has since been changed again to Ansbacher Cayman Limited. The remaining 25% interest was subsequently also sold to the Ansbacher Group. Throughout this report it is referred to as Ansbacher Cayman Limited. The Ansbacher Group has recently been sold to the First National Bank of South Africa.

From the mid-1970's Ansbacher Cayman Limited placed substantial deposits with Guinness & Mahon (Ireland) Limited, which by 1989 had grown to approximately £38 million. These deposits, which it must be emphasised were deposited in the name of Ansbacher Cayman Limited and not of individuals, were made up of monies which had been deposited by persons resident in Ireland with Ansbacher Cayman Limited. Up to the time that Mr. Desmond

Traynor left Guinness & Mahon (Ireland) Limited he organised the deposits in Ansbacher Cayman Limited for the Irish residents and maintained records of those deposits both for his own purposes and for Ansbacher Cayman Limited. Mr. Desmond Traynor was at all times assisted in this by Mr. Padraig Collery, who was responsible for the actual record-keeping, which in latter days were kept on computer. Even after Mr. Desmond Traynor left Guinness & Mahon (Ireland) Limited, he continued to instruct Mr. Padraig Collery to keep the records of the depositors in Ansbacher Cayman Limited. These are the Ansbacher accounts which will be described later in more detail.

Operation of Ansbacher Accounts

As the Tribunal has not yet had access to the files of Ansbacher Cayman Limited, nor to those of the late Mr. John Furze, it is impossible to detail with certainty the workings of the Ansbacher accounts. However, from the evidence of Ms. Sandra Kells of Guinness & Mahon (Ireland) Limited and of Mr. Padraig Collery, together with an internal audit report of a review of Guinness & Mahon (Ireland) Limited conducted in 1989 by its then parent company Guinness Mahon & Co. of London, and a review of the local audit of Ansbacher Cayman Limited by the auditors to Guinness Mahon & Co. in 1987, it is possible to give a broad outline of how the system operated. According to Mr. Padraig Collery the system had been operating since at least the early 1970s.

Mr. Desmond Traynor was both Deputy Chairman of Guinness & Mahon (Ireland) Limited, and its effective Chief Executive, and at the same time was one of the founders of Ansbacher Cayman Limited. While he held these two positions he appears to have acted on behalf of a number of Irish persons who wished to deposit their money off-shore, and this money was deposited in Ansbacher Cayman Limited by Mr. Desmond Traynor on their behalf. In effect, Mr. Desmond Traynor was acting as the Irish agent of Ansbacher Cayman Limited in this regard. It is not clear whether a separate deposit account was opened in Ansbacher Cayman Limited in respect of each of these depositors, or whether the money was all placed in an account in the name of or under the control of Mr. Desmond Traynor, or a combination of both. Whichever way it operated, Mr. Desmond Traynor was the link man, and would take instructions from the clients in Dublin and ensure that they were complied with in Ansbacher Cayman Limited.

At the same time, Ansbacher Cayman Limited deposited the monies which it had received from Irish clients in its own name with Guinness & Mahon (Ireland) Limited. Again, it is not clear whether all such monies were deposited back in Guinness & Mahon (Ireland) Limited, or only a part of them. The arrangement was that Ansbacher Cayman Limited paid to the Irish clients interest calculated at one eighth per cent per annum less than the interest which it received from Guinness & Mahon (Ireland) Limited, thus generating a small profit for Ansbacher Cayman Limited. It is not known in what currency the money was deposited with Ansbacher Cayman Limited by the Irish clients, but most of the Ansbacher Cayman Limited deposits in Guinness & Mahon (Ireland) Limited were in sterling, although there were some deposits in other currencies.

This was a very ingenious system whereby Irish depositors could have their money off-shore, with no record of their deposits in Ireland, and yet obtain an interest rate which was only one eighth of one per cent less than they would have obtained had they deposited it themselves in an Irish bank. It is not the function of this Tribunal to examine these deposits in any detail, and it may well be that a number of the Irish depositors may have been people engaged in international business which was greatly facilitated by having a sterling account abroad which did not require exchange control permission to operate. No doubt there were others who deposited the monies in this way from other motives.

As the client base for these Ansbacher deposits was Irish, it was very important to have the contact person in Ireland. Mr. Desmond Traynor performed that role while he was alive, and while the records of Guinness & Mahon (Ireland) Limited merely recorded a large deposit or a number of large deposits in the name of Ansbacher Cayman Limited, Mr. Desmond Traynor appears to have kept a record of the Irish clients of Ansbacher Cayman Limited whose money had been re-deposited in Guinness & Mahon (Ireland) Limited. These records were referred to as memorandum accounts, that is they were in one sense sub-accounts within the deposit made by Ansbacher Cayman Limited, and a memorandum was kept for each such sub-account. Mr. Padraig Collery, who was particularly skilled at computerising records, was in charge of keeping these memorandum accounts, and according to him, such accounts actually existed when he first joined Guinness & Mahon (Ireland) Limited in 1974. He took over responsibility for keeping the records of these accounts in the late 1970's. These records were kept by reference to codes, and the name of the Irish client did not appear on any of the records. These records were such that they would be a mirror image of records kept by Ansbacher Cayman Limited in the Cayman Islands.

While Mr. Padraig Collery was in charge of keeping the records, during Mr. Desmond Traynor's lifetime, he did not either accept or give instructions in relation to the accounts. He was instructed by Mr. Desmond Traynor to debit or credit specific memorandum accounts. If, for example, one of the customers wanted to withdraw a sum of money, Mr. Desmond Traynor would instruct Mr. Padraig Collery to that effect, a withdrawal would be made, either by cheque or in cash, from the account of Ansbacher Cayman Limited in Guinness & Mahon (Ireland) Limited, and the memorandum accounts kept by Mr. Padraig Collery would be adjusted accordingly. Presumably at the same time the equivalent account of the client with Ansbacher Cayman Limited would be adjusted in the Cayman Islands. It also appears from some of the transactions with which this report is concerned that deposits were made on behalf of a client directly into an account of Ansbacher Cayman Limited, and the

Tribunal has not been able to ascertain whether these were treated as separate deposits by the Irish client in the records of Ansbacher Cayman Limited.

While Mr. Desmond Traynor was Deputy Chairman of Guinness & Mahon (Ireland) Limited, he was in fact acting in a dual capacity in relation to these transactions. In managing the memorandum accounts he was acting on behalf of Ansbacher Cayman Limited. After he left Guinness & Mahon (Ireland) Limited in 1985, Mr. Padraig Collery remained on, and the system operated largely as before. Instructions would be given by Mr. Desmond Traynor to Mr. Padraig Collery in respect of these memorandum accounts, and Mr. Padraig Collery would act on those instructions, and continued to keep the records of the memorandum accounts. It is also interesting to note that when these records became computerised, they were maintained on a bureau system which shared the same hardware as, but was totally independent of, the system of Guinness & Mahon (Ireland) Limited. The system was controlled solely by Mr. Padraig Collery, and had a password which was unknown to the staff of Guinness & Mahon (Ireland) Limited, and accordingly could only be accessed by Mr. Padraig Collery or, presumably, by Mr. Desmond Traynor.

When Guinness Mahon & Co. Limited sold Ansbacher Cayman Limited to its management, it was a condition of the sale that the Ansbacher deposits would be left for a period in Guinness & Mahon (Ireland) Limited, and would be withdrawn only in stages. The reason for this was that by 1989 it appears there was some £38 million deposited by Ansbacher Cayman Limited in Guinness & Mahon (Ireland) Limited, and this in fact represented almost 35% of the liabilities of Guinness & Mahon (Ireland) Limited. If this entire sum had been withdrawn at one time this could have proved fatal for Guinness & Mahon (Ireland) Limited. Accordingly, the funds were withdrawn over a period of about two years, and a considerable portion of those funds were put on deposit by Ansbacher Cayman Limited, or by other Cayman Islands companies as will be described later, with Irish Intercontinental Bank in Dublin, which is a merchant bank rather than a retail bank.

As a further part of the shifting of the deposits, in September 1992 an account was opened on the instructions of Mr. Desmond Traynor in Irish Intercontinental Bank in the name of a company called Hamilton Ross Co. Limited. This was a company registered in the Cayman Islands, which was under the control of Mr. John Furze. Some of the monies in the Ansbacher Cayman Limited account were transferred into the account in the name of Hamilton Ross Co. Limited. Hamilton Ross Co. Limited had different accounts for different currencies. It would appear, although the Tribunal cannot be certain without access to the information in the Cayman Islands, that Mr. John Furze, possibly in anticipation of his departure from Ansbacher Cayman Limited, in effect transferred the Irish clients to a trust company of his own, namely Hamilton Ross Co. Limited, and continued to operate what was a banking service on behalf of those clients, but through Hamilton Ross Co. Limited rather than through Ansbacher Cayman Limited.

It should be said that Guinness Mahon & Co. Limited had been very unhappy with the situation. Its auditors reviewed the 1987 audit of Ansbacher

Cayman Limited, and the relevant extract from the auditor's report is set out in the Eleventh Schedule hereto. In addition, in 1989 Guinness Mahon & Co. Limited carried out an internal audit of Guinness & Mahon (Ireland) Limited, and the relevant extract from that report is set out in the Twelfth Schedule to this report. Both Ms. Sandra Kells on behalf of Guinness & Mahon (Ireland) Limited and Mr. Padraig Collery have confirmed in evidence that these documents are factually accurate.

After the death of Mr. Desmond Traynor in 1994, these accounts, both when they were in the name of Ansbacher Cayman Limited and when they were transferred into the name of Hamilton Ross Co. Limited, continued to be operated by Mr. Padraig Collery. His evidence, which the Tribunal accepts, is that during the lifetime of Mr. Desmond Traynor he acted on the instructions of Mr. Desmond Traynor, and occasionally on those of Mr. John Furze, and that after Mr. Desmond Traynor's death he acted on the instructions of Mr. John Furze.

Poinciana Fund Limited

Poinciana Fund Limited is a trust company registered in the Cayman Islands, which was controlled by Mr. John Furze. Initially, there were deposits in Guinness & Mahon (Ireland) Limited under an account name "Ansbacher Limited re Poinciana Fund Limited". This was an account in the name of Ansbacher Limited but with the description or designation "Poinciana Fund Ltd." Later, accounts in the name of "Poinciana Fund Ltd." were opened although Guinness & Mahon (Ireland) Limited continued to classify these as part of the Ansbacher deposits. Again, without access to documents and information in the Cayman Islands, it is not possible to ascertain the exact purpose of these accounts, or the exact nature of Poinciana Fund Limited. It would appear to be a trust company which held and invested money on behalf of clients, and some of the monies held by it in Guinness & Mahon (Ireland) Limited were held for the benefit of Mr. Charles Haughey. It seems probable that Poinciana Fund Limited deposited its clients monies with Ansbacher Cayman Limited, and they were re-deposited by Ansbacher Cayman Limited in a separate account with Guinness & Mahon (Ireland) Limited. However, within the Poinciana Fund Limited account there were again sub-accounts or memorandum accounts, the records of which, so far as they affected Irish clients, were kept by Mr. Desmond Traynor and Mr. Padraig Collery. These included accounts designated by code by the letters S2 to S9 inclusive. S8 was a sterling account out of which payments were made for the benefit of Mr. Charles Haughey, and S9 was a deutschmark account out of which payments were made for his benefit. When the funds were moved to Irish Intercontinental Bank and the Hamilton Ross Co. Limited account opened, it appears that the Poinciana Fund Limited monies were transferred as part of the Ansbacher Cayman Limited funds transferred to the Hamilton Ross Co. Limited account. The S accounts continued to be operated as sub-accounts of Poinciana Fund Ltd. which itself operated as a sub-account of the Hamilton Ross Co. Limited account. In some cases, separate accounts were opened for such S accounts and in particular, the deutschmark money in the S9 account was held in an account entitled "Hamilton Ross Limited S9". While the S8 memorandum account may have included monies held beneficially for Mr. Charles Haughey and others, the S9 account appears to have been used exclusively for Mr. Haughey's benefit.

Chapter 7

Payments to Mr. Charles Haughey

Initial Approach on Behalf of Mr. Charles Haughey

Some time in late 1987, and probably in early or mid November of that year, Mr. Noel Fox received a telephone call from Mr. Desmond Traynor, who he knew as a fellow accountant and banker, although not very well. Mr. Desmond Traynor told him that he was dealing with a significant problem, a business problem, that related to Mr. Charles Haughey, the then Taoiseach, and that the way he was dealing with the problem was that he was seeking to put together about half a dozen people to contribute £150,000 each towards settling his problem. He did not specify the nature of the problem, but he asked Mr. Noel Fox to approach Mr. Ben Dunne to see if he would become part of the consortium, which Mr. Noel Fox agreed to do.

At that time Mr. Noel Fox was a very close adviser to the Dunnes Stores Group, and attended a management meeting every morning at eight o'clock in the head office of Dunnes Stores at Stephens Street, Dublin. At the next meeting after his conversation with Mr. Desmond Traynor he spoke to Mr. Ben Dunne and told him of the approach. Mr. Ben Dunne's recollection is that he took a few days to consider the matter, and then spoke to Mr. Noel Fox about it after a further morning meeting. Mr. Noel Fox impressed on him the need for confidentiality and on hearing this Mr. Ben Dunne said "I think Haughey is making a huge mistake trying to get six or seven people together .... Christ picked twelve apostles and one of them crucified him".

Mr. Ben Dunne then agreed to pay the entire amount, which he recollects as being about £700,000, while Mr. Noel Fox recollects it as being about £900,000. Mr. Ben Dunne did not offer to pay this immediately, but said that he would be able to pay it in the middle of 1988. Because of the confidentiality, he wished to source the money from abroad.

A short time later, Mr. Noel Fox was again contacted by Mr. Desmond Traynor who said that Mr. Charles Haughey urgently required the sterling equivalent of £205,000, and asked that it be provided by way of a cheque made out to Mr. John Furze, who he said was the banker looking after the transaction. Mr. Noel Fox had never heard of Mr. John Furze, nor did he know what bank he was connected with.

Mr. Noel Fox was contacted on three further occasions by Mr. Desmond Traynor seeking money on behalf of Mr. Charles Haughey. In July 1988 he asked for £471,000 sterling, in April or May 1989 he asked for £150,000 sterling and in February 1990 he asked for a further £200,000 sterling. In each case Mr. Desmond Traynor specified the manner in which the payments were to be made, the name of the payee and the account into which they were to be paid. Mr. Noel Fox in turn passed on each of these requests, with the details given by Mr. Desmond Traynor, to Mr. Ben Dunne, and in each case Mr. Ben Dunne provided the necessary payments. It is proposed to deal with each of these separately.

Payment of £182,630 Sterling

In late November 1987, when the request for the sterling equivalent of £205,000 was made, Mr. Ben Dunne instructed Mr. Noel Fox to contact Mr. Matt Price, Manager at the Bangor County Down branch of Dunnes Stores and to get a sterling cheque from him for this amount. Mr. Noel Fox duly passed on this request to Mr. Matt Price, who verified the request with Mr. Ben Dunne and then drew the cheque on Dunnes Stores (Bangor) Limited No. 4 account at the Newry, Co. Down branch of the Ulster Bank for £182,630 sterling. On the same day, he sent this cheque to Mr. Noel Fox by post, and he in turn passed the cheque on to Mr. Desmond Traynor.

On 8th December 1987 Mr. Desmond Traynor sent the cheque to Guinness Mahon & Co. in London asking them to credit the account of Guinness Mahon Cayman Trust (the then name of Ansbacher Cayman Limited) when the funds were cleared and to send the funds to Guinness Mahon Cayman Trust sub-company account in Guinness & Mahon (Ireland) Limited in Dublin. This request was in fact countermanded by a telephone call, followed by a letter of 11th December 1987 from Mr. Desmond Traynor, on the note paper of Guinness Mahon Cayman Trust Limited, directing that the proceeds of the cheque should be credited to Guinness & Mahon (Ireland) Limited's account with Guinness Mahon & Co. in London. This was done on 17th December 1987, and on the same date Guinness & Mahon (Ireland) Limited's account with Guinness Mahon & Co. in London was debited with the sum of £182,630 sterling, and an account called the sundry sub co. account of Guinness Mahon Cayman Trust Limited with Guinness & Mahon (Ireland) Limited was credited with this sum.

On 1st December 1987, Amiens Investments Limited, a company owned by Mr. Desmond Traynor which had an account with Guinness & Mahon (Ireland) Limited, requested an overdraft facility for that account in the sum of £100,000 for a period of thirty days. This request was approved and on 2nd December 1987 a draft for £105,000 was drawn on Amiens Investments Limited's account in Guinness & Mahon (Ireland) Limited payable to the Agricultural Credit Corporation. On 3rd December 1987 this draft was lodged with the Agricultural Credit Corporation and was applied by them to clear a loan by Agricultural Credit Corporation to Mr. Charles Haughey. This all appears to have been done in anticipation of the receipt of the funds from Mr. Ben Dunne.

On 15th December 1987 the account of Amiens Investment Limited was credited with £204,055.87 from the sundry sub-account of Ansbacher Cayman Limited, this being the then Irish pound equivalent of £182,630 sterling.

Thus the entire proceeds of the cheque given by Mr. Ben Dunne was paid into the account of Amiens Investments Limited. Out of this account, £105,000 was paid to discharge Mr. Charles Haughey's debt to the Agricultural Credit Corporation. Of the balance, on 22nd December 1987, £59,000 was withdrawn by two withdrawals in cash. No receipt exists for these withdrawals, which means that the money must have been withdrawn by somebody very well known to the bank or by somebody in the bank. The probability is that the money was withdrawn in cash by Mr. Desmond Traynor and given to Mr. Charles Haughey. On 18th December 1987 a sum of £30,000 was debited to the Amiens Investments Limited account and on 22nd December 1987 a sum of £10,000 was debited to that account. A few days later sums of £30,000 and £10,000 were credited to the Haughey Boland No. 3 account, which is the client account of Haughey Boland, and as will be seen later, was the account used at that time by Haughey Boland to make payments to or on behalf of Mr. Charles Haughey. It thus appears that the entire proceeds of the cheque for £182,630 sterling was applied for the benefit of Mr. Charles Haughey.

Payment of £471,000 Sterling

This sum was requested by Mr. Desmond Traynor some time in July 1988. Mr. Desmond Traynor asked that the money be paid into an account in Barclays Bank plc at 68 Knightsbridge, London for the credit of J. Furze.

Mr. Ben Dunne had funds available to him which appear to be profits generated by Dunnes Stores transactions in the Far East, and these funds were managed by a Swiss trust company called Equifex Trust Corporation AG in Zug Switzerland, which, insofar as Mr. Ben Dunne's funds were concerned, took its instructions from Mr. Julian Harper of European Corporate Services Limited, an Isle of Man company used by Mr. Ben Dunne for managing some of his financial affairs. Mr. Ben Dunne arranged that £471,000 sterling would be transferred from these funds through a firm of lawyers in Switzerland. On 1st August 1988 the sum of £470,994.09 sterling was transferred from Credit Suisse in Zurich to the account of Mr. John Furze at Barclays Bank plc in Knightsbridge, London. On 3rd August 1988 this sum was transferred by telegraphic transfer to the account of Guinness & Mahon (Ireland) Limited in Guinness Mahon & Co. in London and on 5th August 1988 the same sum was transferred from Guinness & Mahon (Ireland) Limited's account in Guinness Mahon & Co. in London to an account of Ansbacher Cayman Limited with Guinness & Mahon (Ireland) Limited known as the Ansbacher Cayman Sundry Sub Co. Account. On 10th August 1988 the same sum was transferred from the Ansbacher Cayman Sundry Sub Co. Account to the Ansbacher Cayman Call Deposit Account in Guinness & Mahon (Ireland) Limited, which was a general deposit account of funds of Ansbacher Cayman Limited.

Payment of £150,000 Sterling

In late April 1989 Mr. Desmond Traynor again contacted Mr. Noel Fox requesting a further £150,000 sterling, and again Mr. Noel Fox passed this request on to Mr. Ben Dunne. Mr. Ben Dunne arranged for this payment to be made from the same source as the earlier payment of £471,000 sterling, again following the instructions given by Mr. Desmond Traynor. His instructions this time were that the money was to be transferred into the account of Henry Ansbacher & Company Limited in the Royal Bank of Scotland in Threadneedle Street in London for further credit to account number 190017-202. This latter account transpired to be the sterling call deposit account of Ansbacher Cayman Limited with Henry Ansbacher & Company Limited in London. On 8th May 1989 the sum of £149,996 sterling was credited to the said sterling call deposit account of Ansbacher Cayman Limited. The same sum was debited to the Ansbacher Cayman Limited Sundry Sub Co. Account. Just why the transaction was handled in this rather convoluted way is not clear, but Ms. Sandra Kells from Guinness & Mahon (Ireland) Limited gave evidence that the most likely explanation is that Mr. Padraig Collery, who handled the transaction, made an initial error as to which of the Ansbacher accounts should have been credited with the money, and later sought to reverse part of the transaction. This seems a likely explanation. In any event there then appears to have been some confusion between the banks, but the net effect is that on 13th June 1989 the Ansbacher Cayman Limited call deposit account with Henry Ansbacher & Company Limited was debited with £149,996 sterling and the Ansbacher Cayman Limited call deposit account with Guinness & Mahon (Ireland) Limited was credited with £149,996 sterling.

Payment of £200,000 Sterling

In February 1990 Mr. Desmond Traynor again approached Mr. Noel Fox seeking a further £200,000 for Mr. Charles Haughey. Again, he gave Mr. Noel Fox particulars of the account into which it was to be paid, and Mr. Noel Fox passed on the request and the particulars to Mr. Ben Dunne, who again agreed to make the payment.

On this occasion, Mr. Ben Dunne directed that the payment be made out of the account of Tutbury Limited at Rea Brothers (Isle of Man) Limited. On 1st March 1990 the account of Ansbacher Cayman Limited with Henry Ansbacher & Company Limited in London was credited with £200,000 sterling from Tutbury Limited.

On 12th March 1990 the account of Ansbacher Cayman Limited with Henry Ansbacher & Company Limited was debited with the £200,000 sterling and the account of Guinness & Mahon (Ireland) Limited with Guinness Mahon & Co. in London was credited with the same sum. On 14th March 1990 this account was debited with the £200,000 sterling, and the Ansbacher Cayman Limited call deposit account with Guinness & Mahon (Ireland) Limited was credited with this sum.

Effect of These Transactions

The initial payment of £182,630 sterling appears to have been dispersed in its entirety for the benefit of Mr. Charles Haughey. £105,000 was used to discharge his liabilities to Agricultural Credit Corporation, £40,000 was paid into the Haughey Boland client account, which account provided funds for the benefit of Mr. Haughey, and £59,000 was withdrawn in cash. The Tribunal considers that the proper inference is that this money was given in cash to Mr. Charles Haughey. The monies from the other three payments all finally ended up in the call deposit account of Ansbacher Cayman Limited with Guinness & Mahon (Ireland) Limited, which was the general account of Ansbacher Cayman Limited with Guinness & Mahon (Ireland) Limited. Presumably these sums were then credited to one of the memorandum accounts already referred to.

Payment of £210,000 Sterling

In early November 1991 Mr. Ben Dunne asked his solicitor Mr. Noel Smyth to get three bank drafts for him of £70,000 sterling each from Tutbury Limited in the Isle of Man. These drafts were to be in fictitious names and were not at that time intended by Mr. Ben Dunne to be paid for Mr. Charles Haughey's benefit. Mr. Ben Dunne has said that they were drawn for personal reasons, and the Tribunal did not consider it necessary to explore what these were. Mr. Noel Smyth duly gave instructions for the drafts to be obtained and they were drawn on 13th November 1991 on the account of Tutbury Limited in Rea Brothers (Isle of Man) Limited and delivered by courier to Mr. Noel Smyth. He in turn handed these drafts to Mr. Ben Dunne.

Mr. Ben Dunne's evidence is that some days later he was playing golf at Baltray and he had the three bank drafts in his pocket. After the game of golf he telephoned Mr. Charles Haughey and it was arranged that he would call in to Mr. Charles Haughey's house on his way home. He did so, and got the impression that Mr. Charles Haughey was not himself but looked down and depressed. As he was leaving he took the three bank drafts out of his pocket and handed them to Mr. Charles Haughey and said "Look, that is something for yourself". Mr. Charles Haughey responded "Thank you big fellow".

Mr. Charles Haughey's evidence is that he has no recollection of this incident at all, but he does accept that he did personally get the three bank drafts from Mr. Ben Dunne, and he accepts that the proceeds of the bank drafts were used for his benefit.

Mr. Charles Haughey probably sent the three bank drafts to Mr. Desmond Traynor and on 22nd November 1991 Mr. Desmond Traynor's secretary sent one of the bank drafts to Irish Intercontinental Bank for the credit of the general account of Ansbacher Cayman Limited with Irish Intercontinental Bank. On 27th November 1991 she sent a second draft with the same instructions and on 2nd December 1991 she sent the third draft with the same instructions. Thus the entire £210,000 was lodged with the general account of Ansbacher Cayman Limited in Irish Intercontinental Bank.

Position of Dunnes Stores Group

There is no doubt that most of the payments made by Mr. Ben Dunne which come within the ambit of this Report were made out of accounts which he solely controlled. The Tribunal accepts that for the most part the other directors were unaware of these payments, and indeed in many cases unaware of the existence of the accounts.

However, the Board of the Dunnes Holding Company chose to entrust the financial affairs of the Group to Mr. Ben Dunne, and chose to give him very wide and unsupervised powers. It is not for this Report to examine the relationship between Mr. Ben Dunne and the Dunnes Stores Group, but as a matter of general principle the Tribunal feels that it must state that prima facie the Board of Directors of a company is responsible for the actions of the person they choose as Managing Director, at least where he has ostensible authority to act on behalf of the company. At the very least, the company must bear some blame for not having put any proper supervisory procedure in place.

Payments to Mr. Charles Haughey

For very many years prior to 1991 Mr. Charles Haughey's day to day financial affairs were dealt with by his former accountancy firm of Haughey Boland. They carried out what is described by Mr. Paul Carty of that firm as a book-keeping function. Mr. Charles Haughey's secretary would send all his bills to Haughey Boland for payment. They would pay these bills by way of cheque drawn on their client account. A separate cheque book was kept purely for Mr. Charles Haughey's affairs, and proper books were kept detailing the payments. When funds were needed to make these payments, Haughey Boland applied to Mr. Desmond Traynor who provided the funds, frequently by way of a bank draft drawn on Guinness & Mahon (Ireland) Limited. Mr. Paul Carty of Haughey Boland has given evidence that they did not know the source of the funds other than that they were paid through Mr. Desmond Traynor.

From the records kept by Haughey Boland, the Tribunal has established that the following payments were made on behalf of Mr. Charles Haughey from 1st August 1988, being the date of the first payment by Mr. Ben Dunne, until 31st January 1991, when Haughey Boland ceased to act. These payments were:—

1st August 1988 to 31st December 1988 — £103,850

1st January 1989 to 31st December 1989 — £325,000

1st January 1990 to 31st December 1990 — £264,000

1st January 1991 to 31st January 1991 — £16,000

Thus the total of the payments made on behalf of Mr. Charles Haughey during this period was £708,850.

At the end of 1991 Haughey Boland became part of the much larger firm of Deloitte & Touche, and before this took place Mr. Paul Carty had a meeting with Mr. Desmond Traynor. Mr. Desmond Traynor said that he would like to see a more personal approach to Mr. Charles Haughey's financial affairs, rather than have them dealt with by a very large firm. Shortly afterwards he contacted Mr. Paul Carty and told him that Mr. Jack Stakelum would be taking over, and a meeting was held between Mr. Paul Carty, Mr. Desmond Traynor and Mr. Jack Stakelum when the arrangements for the transfer of the function were finalised. In January 1991 Mr. Jack Stakelum was given all necessary books and records.

Mr. Jack Stakelum had formerly been a partner in Haughey Boland, which firm he left in November 1975 to set up his own financial consultancy practice, which he still carries on under the name of Business Enterprises Limited. He was a close personal friend of Mr. Desmond Traynor and has told the Tribunal that he was asked to take over Mr. Charles Haughey's affairs because they required confidentiality. Instead of using his own client account, he opened a separate bank account purely to deal with Mr. Charles Haughey's financial affairs, and he appears to have had a slightly more limited function in the paying of bills than Haughey Boland had, in that he did not deal with wages of all persons employed by Mr. Charles Haughey. This function appears to have continued to be carried out by Deloitte & Touche, who also continued to look after Mr. Charles Haughey's tax affairs.

At the beginning, Mr. Jack Stakelum kept a monthly analysis of the payments made and showed them to Mr. Charles Haughey from time to time. He said that Mr. Charles Haughey took no interest whatever in these analyses and did not even look at them, and after some months Mr. Jack Stakelum ceased this practice, as it appeared to him to be pointless.

The actual system operated by Mr. Jack Stakelum was the same as that operated by Haughey Boland, namely that the bills would be sent in by Mr. Charles Haughey's secretary, and when money was required it would be obtained from Mr. Desmond Traynor. Mr. Jack Stakelum has given evidence that he never asked Mr. Desmond Traynor where the money came from, as he felt that the whole matter was totally confidential.

After the death of Mr. Desmond Traynor, Mr. Jack Stakelum approached Mr. Padraig Collery, and asked whether he would continue to make payments from the same source. Before doing so, Mr. Padraig Collery checked with Mr. John Furze that this was in order. Mr. Padraig Collery was still keeping the memorandum accounts, and he was aware that the payments during Mr. Desmond Traynor's lifetime had come out of either an account designated S8, which was a sterling account, or an account designated S9 which was a deutschmark account. When Mr. Padraig Collery took over making the payments himself, he made them out of the S8 account if there was sufficient funds, and otherwise he made them out of the S9 account. At some stage, Mr. Jack Stakelum made him aware that these funds were being paid for the benefit of Mr. Charles Haughey, although the Tribunal believes he was probably already aware of this.

The Ansbacher Files

Mr. Desmond Traynor had an office at 42 Fitzwilliam Square Dublin, which was provided for him by CRH plc, of which he was the Chairman. He held all the records relating to the Ansbacher Cayman Limited accounts in this office, and while the computer records appear to have been maintained by Mr. Padraig Collery, the actual files were kept by Mr. Desmond Traynor.

Mr. John Furze attended Mr. Desmond Traynor's funeral in Dublin, and spoke to Mr. Padraig Collery and asked him to assist in locating the files relating to Ansbacher Cayman Limited. As Mr. Padraig Collery considered that these files belonged to Ansbacher Cayman Limited, he removed them from Mr. Desmond Traynor's office and kept the files in the office of a friend. Towards the end of 1994 Mr. John Furze returned to Dublin and did a full review of all the files. He took some files back with him to Cayman and destroyed others which he said were no longer relevant. However, he appears to have left a number of active files dealing with the memorandum accounts with Mr. Padraig Collery at that stage.

When Mr. John Furze left Ansbacher Cayman Limited at the end of 1995, he again visited Dublin. He had ceased to have any connection with Ansbacher Cayman Limited, but of course he still controlled Hamilton Ross Co. Limited which maintained funds in Irish Intercontinental Bank. Mr. Padraig Collery's evidence is that in December 1995 he ceased to be a signatory on the Ansbacher Cayman Limited account. His evidence is that he consulted officials of Ansbacher Cayman Limited, and, by agreement with them, destroyed many of the files. It does seem clear, that copies of these files still exist in the hands of Ansbacher Cayman Limited in the Cayman Islands.

Mr. Ben Dunne / Mr. Charles Haughey Relationship

It appears from all the evidence that Mr. Ben Dunne was an impetuously generous person. This is shown, for example, by his immediate reaction to the request for funds for the Fine Gael Party, and also by his actions in relation to the donation to Mrs. Mary Robinson's presidential campaign. However, it is difficult to explain his relationship with Mr. Charles Haughey solely by reference to impetuous generosity. When approached by Mr. Noel Fox, he was told that there was an urgent need for a large sum of money, which he agreed to provide. However, while he almost immediately provided the first payment of £182,630 sterling, he promised to pay what was probably the balance of £700,000 in some months time. He then proceeded to make elaborate arrangements for the transfer of funds from the Far East through a firm of lawyers in Switzerland, which was certainly not a spontaneous act. He made similar complicated arrangements in relation to the third and fourth payments.

The evidence also is that, at the time of the initial request, Mr. Ben Dunne had only a casual acquaintanceship with Mr. Charles Haughey. After the first payment was made, his contacts with Mr. Charles Haughey became much more frequent, although the payment and receipt of the monies remained an unspoken bond between them. Mr. Ben Dunne's evidence is that he thought it quite wrong that the Taoiseach of the country should be facing financial problems, and that he had a very high regard for Mr. Charles Haughey's ability. While the Tribunal has no doubt as to the truth of this evidence, it is hardly sufficient in itself to explain the generosity shown by Mr. Ben Dunne.

It is no part of the function of the Tribunal to conduct a psychological study of Mr. Ben Dunne. However, it does appear to the Tribunal that a possible motive for the actions of Mr. Ben Dunne, in the absence of any ulterior political motive, was simply to buy the friendship, or at least the acquaintance, of a person in a very powerful political position. Mr. Ben Dunne appears to have had many friends in the business community, but few, if any, in the political community.

Motives of Payments to Mr. Charles Haughey

The Tribunal has made extensive enquiries throughout the public service as to any possible instances in which Mr. Charles Haughey might have used his influence for the benefit of either Mr. Ben Dunne personally, the Dunne family or the Dunnes Stores Group. The only request for special favours which the Tribunal has been able to uncover was a request by Mr. Ben Dunne for a personal meeting with the Chairman of the Revenue Commissioners. The Tribunal has heard evidence of this meeting, and is quite satisfied that it was merely a routine meeting, at which nothing specific was requested by Mr. Ben Dunne. The Tribunal is also quite satisfied that the only part played in the meeting by Mr. Charles Haughey was to actually arrange it, but that no representations were made by Mr. Charles Haughey on behalf of Mr. Ben Dunne or the Dunnes Stores Group. The Tribunal is satisfied that there was no wrongful use of his position by Mr. Charles Haughey in this regard.

Apart from this, the Tribunal has found no evidence of any favours asked of Mr. Charles Haughey by Mr. Ben Dunne, the Dunne family or the Dunnes Stores Group, nor has it found any evidence of any attempt by Mr. Charles Haughey to exercise his influence for the benefit of Mr. Ben Dunne, the Dunne family or the Dunnes Stores Group.

Notwithstanding the fact that there appears to have been no political impropriety involved, the Tribunal considers it quite unacceptable that Mr. Charles Haughey, or indeed any member of the Oireachtas, should receive personal gifts of this nature, particularly from prominent businessmen within the State. It is even more unacceptable that Mr. Charles Haughey's whole life style should be dependant upon such gifts, as would appear to be the case. If such gifts were to be permissible, the potential for bribery and corruption would be enormous.

If politicians are to give an effective service to all their constituents, or to all the citizens of the State, they must not be under a financial obligation to some constituents or some citizens only. By allowing himself to be put in a position of dependency, Mr. Charles Haughey failed in his obligations to his constituents and to the citizens of this State, and indeed has devalued some of the undoubtedly valuable work which he did when in office.

Chapter 8

Mr. Ciaran Haughey / Celtic Helicopters Limited

Payment by Mr. Ben Dunne to Mr. Ciaran Haughey

Mr. Ciaran Haughey is a son of Mr. Charles Haughey and is a director of and a substantial shareholder in Celtic Helicopters Limited, which is engaged in the general charter of helicopters. He is also a professional helicopter pilot. Celtic Helicopters Limited was incorporated in 1985, and from an early stage did a considerable amount of business with the Dunnes Stores Group. On 21st October 1988 Mr. Ben Dunne gave to Mr. Ciaran Haughey a cheque for £10,000 drawn on the account of the Marino Dublin branch of the Bank of Ireland and made payable to cash. Mr. Ben Dunne and Mr. Ciaran Haughey have given two totally different accounts of the background to this payment.

Mr. Ben Dunne has given evidence that Mr. Ciaran Haughey personally piloted the helicopter which he used and did a lot of flying for him, putting in long hours, and that he made this payment to him on top of any payments he was giving for the hire of the helicopter. It would seem, according to this account, that this was in effect a bonus payment to Mr. Ciaran Haughey personally, in much the same way as Mr. Ben Dunne made bonus payments to Mr. Michael Lowry.

On the other hand, Mr. Ciaran Haughey's account of this payment is that it was for what he called a "consultancy service", and that Mr. Ben Dunne had asked him to look at different types of helicopters to see which would be best suited to his needs. He further said that about that time he was actually in America doing a course with Bell Helicopters, and he located what he felt might be a suitable helicopter either for Mr. Ben Dunne or some other customers, and he travelled to have a look at it. However, when he was pressed, Mr. Ciaran Haughey accepted that there was nothing in writing in relation to the alleged consultancy, that he had never sent an account to Mr. Ben Dunne, nor had he given a receipt. The Tribunal also considers it very significant that the payment was made out of the account at the Marino Dublin branch of the Bank of Ireland, which is an account which appears to have been used by Mr. Ben Dunne for making personal payments. If this payment had been for consultancy work done for Dunnes Stores, presumably the payment would have been made in the normal way out of one of their trading accounts. The Tribunal has no doubt that Mr. Ben Dunne's account of the events is the correct one, and this was in the nature of a bonus payment to Mr. Ciaran Haughey personally.

Celtic Helicopters Limited

On four occasions funds from the Ansbacher deposits were used to support debts of Celtic Helicopters Limited, and in one case a bank loan was actually repaid out of the Ansbacher deposits. In each case the arrangements were made by Mr. Desmond Traynor.

In March 1991 Guinness & Mahon (Ireland) Limited granted a loan of £100,000 to Celtic Helicopters Limited. This was originally intended to be in the nature of a bridging loan to help to finance the erection of a hanger at Dublin Airport which was to be ultimately financed by Irish Permanent Building Society. The loan was secured by personal guarantees from Mr. Ciaran Haughey and Mr. John Barnicle, co-director and shareholder of Celtic Helicopters Limited. These personal guarantees were in turn secured or backed by a deposit of £100,000 sterling taken from the Ansbacher Cayman Limited general account with Guinness & Mahon (Ireland) Limited and separately deposited to act as security. In evidence, Mr. Ciaran Haughey denied any knowledge of this deposit.

In May 1991 a loan of £150,000 was negotiated for Celtic Helicopters Limited by Mr Desmond Traynor from Irish Intercontinental Bank. £100,000 of this was used to discharge the liability to Guinness & Mahon (Ireland) Limited and the balance went into the general account of Celtic Helicopters Limited. Again, Mr. Ciaran Haughey and Mr. John Barnicle signed letters of guarantee and in addition the sum of £175,000 sterling was transferred from the Ansbacher Cayman Limited general account with Irish Intercontinental Bank to a special deposit account in that bank to be held as security for the loan. This money was in fact taken out of the S8 account, which is a sterling memorandum account held on behalf of Mr. Charles Haughey. In mid February 1992 the loan was repaid on the instructions of Mr. Desmond Traynor out of the Ansbacher Cayman Limited general deposit with Irish Intercontinental Bank, and the monies which had been placed in the special deposit account were released back into the Ansbacher Cayman Limited general account. Again, Mr. Ciaran Haughey in evidence has denied any knowledge of the use of the Ansbacher funds to secure or repay this loan.

The working account of Celtic Helicopters Limited was with the Dublin Airport branch of the Bank of Ireland, and by March 1992 it was overdrawn to the extent of approximately £100,000. The bank required security for an overdraft at this level, and Mr. Desmond Traynor arranged a guarantee from Irish Intercontinental Bank to secure the overdraft. Irish Intercontinental Bank were paid a fee of 1% per annum in respect of the guarantee, and they also obtained counter guarantees from Mr. Ciaran Haughey and Mr. John Barnicle. Again, the sum of £100,000 sterling was taken from the Ansbacher general account, and in particular from the S8 memorandum account of Mr. Charles Haughey, and deposited with Irish Intercontinental Bank as security for the directors' guarantees. Subsequently this was replaced by a deposit for the same sum by Hamilton Ross Co. Limited. It is believed that this loan has recently been repaid by the company, and the monies on deposit have been released back to Hamilton Ross Co. Limited.

Finally, in April 1993 Celtic Helicopters Limited negotiated the purchase of a helicopter from a Swiss company called Jet Aviation Business Jets. The vendors required a deposit of 75,000 US dollars but agreed to accept a guarantee for that sum from Irish Intercontinental Bank in lieu of a cash deposit. By this stage much of the monies with which this report is concerned which had been deposited with Irish Intercontinental Bank by Ansbacher Cayman Limited had in fact been transferred to Hamilton Ross Co. Limited, and monies were taken from the Hamilton Ross Co. Limited deposit to secure the guarantee given by Irish Intercontinental Bank. In this case the monies were taken from the S9 memorandum account, which is the deutschmark deposit account held on behalf of Mr. Charles Haughey. In due course the purchase of the helicopter was commercially financed, and the guarantee of Irish Intercontinental Bank was released.

Mr. Ciaran Haughey has denied all knowledge of the Ansbacher Cayman Limited or Hamilton Ross Co. Limited funds or of their use to support Celtic Helicopters Limited. His evidence is that all arrangements were made on behalf of the company by Mr. Desmond Traynor, and that the backing transactions were never explained to him. In support of this, it is undoubtedly a fact that the facility letters in respect of the three bank loans make no mention of a back to back deposit to secure the loans, but simply rely on the personal guarantees of the directors as security. The Tribunal accepts that it is a possibility that Mr. Desmond Traynor made the backing arrangements without the knowledge of Mr. Ciaran Haughey, but the Tribunal cannot accept that the loan of £150,000 was actually paid off out of these monies without such knowledge. The Tribunal cannot accept that directors of a company would not be aware that a loan of this magnitude from a bank to the company had been discharged, not out of the funds of the company, but by a third party.

Chapter 9

Evidence of Mr. Charles Haughey

On 15th July 1997 Mr. Charles Haughey gave evidence to the Tribunal, having first read the statement set out in the ninth schedule to this report. In the course of that statement and of his subsequent evidence he made a number of statements of fact which call for comment. Regrettably, in relation to many of these matters, the Tribunal considers Mr. Charles Haughey's evidence to be unacceptable and untrue. In particular, the following matters call for comment:—

1. His evidence was that Mr. Desmond Traynor managed his financial affairs since about 1960 with complete discretion to act on his behalf without reference back to him. He accepts that there was always a flow of money coming which was used to defray his living and domestic expenses, but claims never to have asked Mr. Desmond Traynor how he managed his affairs or to have discussed in detail the arrangements he was making. He further alleges that he does not recollect ever signing any documents in relation to his affairs.

    If Mr. Desmond Traynor managed his affairs for over 30 years it is quite unbelievable that all financial decisions over that period were taken by Mr. Desmond Traynor without any reference to Mr. Charles Haughey. There must have been serious financial decisions which had to be made during that period which no financial advisor would take without reference back to his principal.

2. Mr. Desmond Traynor did indicate that there was some financial stringency in 1986/87. Mr. Charles Haughey's evidence is that he did not enquire as to the nature of the stringency or as to how it would be resolved.

    This confirms the evidence of Mr. Noel Fox that Mr. Desmond Traynor told him that there was a significant problem and he was seeking to put together about half a dozen people to contribute £150,000 each towards settling the problem. If this amount of money was needed, there clearly was a serious financial problem, although the Tribunal has only been able to identify debts of just under £400,000 which were paid off around that period. If the problem was so serious as to require almost £1,000,000 it is quite unbelievable that Mr. Desmond Traynor would not have told Mr. Charles Haughey in some detail of the difficulties, and it is equally unbelievable that Mr. Charles Haughey would not have asked.

3. Mr. Charles Haughey does acknowledge that he was aware of the loan from Agricultural Credit Corporation and that it was discharged, and stated that he felt it ought to be paid off when he came into office as Taoiseach because he should not be seen to be indebted to a semi-State bank.

It seems strange that he was aware of this loan, while he does not admit to being aware of any other loans. Furthermore, if his motive in paying it off was to ensure that he was not indebted to a semi-State bank, the question must be raised as to how he knew he was not indebted to any other semi-State body.

4. He accepts Mr. Ben Dunne's evidence that he was handed three bank drafts each for £70,000 sterling by Mr. Ben Dunne in November 1991 but claims to have no recollection of the meeting and to have made no further enquiries.

It is not believable that a person would not remember an event such as this, which was quite bizarre. Furthermore, it is not merely the meeting that would be memorable, as once Mr. Charles Haughey got the three bank drafts he had to do something with them, and as they found their way into Mr. Desmond Traynor's hands and then into the Ansbacher deposits, he presumably must have given them to Mr. Desmond Traynor. It is also most unlikely that if Mr. Charles Haughey gave these bank drafts to Mr. Desmond Traynor, Mr. Desmond Traynor did not reveal that other monies had been received from Mr. Ben Dunne at an earlier date.

5. Mr. Charles Haughey's evidence is that he first learned of the payment of the £1.3 million pounds for his benefit in July 1993, shortly after he had been questioned about it by Mrs. Margaret Heffernan. He says that he did not discuss it in detail with Mr. Desmond Traynor but simply accepted the fact of the gift, and he never discussed it with Mr. Ben Dunne.

If one accepts that this was the first time that Mr. Charles Haughey was made aware of Mr. Ben Dunne's payments, it must have come as an enormous shock to him. Indeed, he acknowledges that he was very disturbed by the information. It is incomprehensible that he would not have asked such further questions as, for example, what the money had been used for, whether it had all been spent or how it had been invested. Even by Mr. Charles Haughey's standards this was a very large sum of money.

6. His evidence also is that he never discussed the tax implications of receiving a gift of £1.3 million pounds, but assumed that Mr. Desmond Traynor would look after that side of it.

   Mr. Charles Haughey was a Chartered Accountant and a former Minister for Finance. He must have been intimately familiar with the provisions of the Capital Acquisitions Tax Act, and been aware that a gift of this nature would give rise to an enormous tax liability. The Tribunal does not believe that this was not discussed between Mr. Charles Haughey and Mr. Desmond Traynor, but believes it far more likely that, not only was it discussed, but that it was decided that the money should be kept off-shore and that its receipt should never be acknowledged. This would be far more consistent with his subsequent actions.

7. He gave evidence that he did not know that Mr. Desmond Traynor was arranging substantial sums of money for him, but then went on to say that he always knew in the back of his mind that Abbeville was there should it be needed.

   While he may not have known the exact sums of money which he was spending, he must have known that large sums of money were being spent on his behalf, despite his denial of having a lavish lifestyle.

8. He professed to know nothing of the affairs of Celtic Helicopters Limited, or in particular that the Ansbacher deposits were used to benefit Celtic Helicopters Limited.

   It is most unlikely that Mr. Desmond Traynor, who appears to have been a meticulously careful person, would have used any of the monies in the Ansbacher deposits which were held for the benefit of Mr. Charles Haughey to support Celtic Helicopters Limited unless he had the authority of Mr. Charles Haughey to do so. Mr. Desmond Traynor had collected the money from Mr. Ben Dunne specifically for the support of Mr. Charles Haughey, and it certainly was not intended by the donor to be used to benefit Mr. Ciaran Haughey or Celtic Helicopters Limited.

9. His evidence was that when Mr. Desmond Traynor died, Mr. Jack Stakelum took over the running of his affairs and the arrangement continued as before. Although he was friendly with Mr. Jack Stakelum,

he said he did not discuss the matter with him and did not enquire into it.

It is factually incorrect to say that Mr. Jack Stakelum took over his affairs. In fact Mr. Jack Stakelum merely continued the existing practice of acting as book-keeper to Mr. Charles Haughey. The running of Mr. Charles Haughey's finances was actually taken over by Mr. Padraig Collery, acting under the instructions of Mr. John Furze. It is beyond all credability that Mr. Charles Haughey, when his financial advisor for thirty years died, would not have become very concerned as to his affairs, and particularly concerned to ensure that his assets were secured. He also does not explain how Mr. Jack Stakelum would have been in a position to take over his affairs, or how he would have known how those affairs were managed. Indeed, the Tribunal is quite satisfied that Mr. Jack Stakelum did not have any knowledge of Mr. Charles Haughey's affairs, other than acting as a book-keeper for him, and that he merely received sums of money, initially from Mr. Desmond Traynor and subsequently from Mr. Padraig Collery, out of which to discharge Mr. Charles Haughey's debts.

10. When asked by the Chairman of the Tribunal whether he discussed with Mr. Desmond Traynor whether the money from Mr. Ben Dunne was all spent or whether some of it was still there, Mr. Charles Haughey gave the answer:

"No. I mean, he would have been supplying the statements of account in that regard".

The clear implication is, that despite his earlier denials, Mr. Charles Haughey had in fact received statements dealing with his accounts which he read and noted, and therefore he did not have to ask about his affairs, because he was already aware of them. The Tribunal believes this to be the true state of affairs.

11. He denied all knowledge of the Ansbacher accounts, and goes so far as to say that he still does not know anything about them.

While the Tribunal has no direct evidence, in the absence of access to documents and information in the Cayman Islands, that Mr. Charles Haughey was aware of the Ansbacher Cayman Limited account, or that Mr. Ben Dunne's money had been paid into such an account, the Tribunal thinks it probable that he was at all times aware that money was being held for his benefit in Ansbacher Cayman Limited. In any event, the Tribunal believes that he must have been made aware of these accounts at the time of the death of Mr.

Desmond Traynor, because the Tribunal believes he must have made enquiries at that time. Furthermore, it is quite unbelievable that he still knows nothing of those accounts. In his opening remarks to this Tribunal on 21st April 1997, Mr. Denis McCullough SC set out in detail the fact that approximately £1.1 million pounds of the monies paid by Mr. Ben Dunne were deposited with Ansbacher Cayman Limited. Even if one accepts Mr. Charles Haughey's evidence that he knew nothing of the Ansbacher Cayman Limited deposits until the opening of this Tribunal, it is quite incredible to think that he would not have made immediate enquiries from Ansbacher Cayman Limited or from Mr. John Furze as to the situation. Unfortunately the Tribunal has not been able to verify this because of the problems in obtaining evidence in the Cayman Islands.

Chapter 10

Offence by Mr. Charles Haughey

Section 1(2) of the Tribunals of Inquiry (Evidence) Act 1921 as amended by the Tribunals of Inquiry (Evidence) (Amendment) Act 1979 includes the following provision:—

> "If a person .... by act or omission, obstructs or hinders the Tribunal in the performance of its functions .... the person shall be guilty of an offence"

On 3rd March 1997 a letter in standard form was sent by the Registrar to the Tribunal to every person who was known to the Tribunal to have been a member of either House of the Oireachtas between 1st January 1986 and 31st December 1996, including Mr. Charles Haughey. By letter dated 7th March 1997 Mr. Charles Haughey replied denying that either he or any connected person or relative of his as defined in the Ethics in Public Office Act 1995 received any payment in cash or in kind of the nature referred to in the Terms of Reference of the Tribunal other than contributions to Mrs. Maureen Haughey, Mr. Ciaran Haughey, Fr. Eoghan Haughey and Mr. Sean Haughey TD. This letter also enclosed copy correspondence between Matheson Ormsby Prentice, Solicitors to the Dunnes Stores Group and Mr. Charles Haughey in November and December 1994, in the course of which correspondence he specifically denied the receipt of any monies from Mr. Ben Dunne.

When the Tribunal received Mr. Ben Dunne's original statement, the Solicitor to the Tribunal wrote to Mr. Charles Haughey on 27th March 1997 enclosing an extract from that statement referring to the payments alleged to have been made to Mr. Charles Haughey and raising certain queries in relation to possible debts of Mr. Charles Haughey which might have been discharged out of these payments. The Solicitor to the Tribunal also asked Mr. Charles Haughey to furnish a statement dealing with the various transactions outlined by Mr. Ben Dunne. A reminder was sent on 2nd April 1997 and a reply was received from Mr. Charles Haughey dated 3rd April 1997. This letter raised certain queries by Mr. Charles Haughey, and contained the statement:—

> "It is suggested that the accompanying documents support the said allegations and with respect to the Tribunal I venture to suggest that a careful perusal of these documents on their own does not corroborate the allegations being made against me".

The Solicitor to the Tribunal replied the same day, saying:—

> "In your letter, you refer to allegations being made against you and to the fact that evidence may be adduced against you. I should make clear that there is no allegation being made by any person to date that in receiving the money in question (either directly or indirectly) you are guilty of any wrong doing or any breach of law. Neither is it being alleged that the money in question was paid to you or for your benefit for an improper purpose or with an improper motive or was received by you for an improper purpose or an improper motive."

After some correspondence, and the making of an Order for Discovery by the Tribunal against Mr. Charles Haughey, an Affidavit of Discovery was sworn by him and furnished to the Tribunal on 18th April 1997. This Affidavit disclosed the correspondence with Matheson Ormsby Prentice referred to in his original letter.

On 19th April 1997 the Solicitor to the Tribunal again wrote to Mr. Charles Haughey requesting the information sought in the letter of 27th March, and this was acknowledged by Mr. Charles Haughey by letter dated 21st April 1997 in which he said, inter alia, it was his intention to co-operate with the Tribunal of Inquiry at all times in accordance with his legal obligations. However, none of the information requested was furnished. As already stated, on 25th April Mr. Noel Smyth raised a legal question as to the admissibility of certain evidence proposed to be given by him of conversations with Mr. Charles Haughey and on 28th April 1997 Mr. Charles Haughey was granted limited representation to deal with the issue of the admissibility of Mr. Noel Smyth's evidence. On 29th April, the Solicitor to the Tribunal wrote to the Solicitors representing Mr. Charles Haughey asking would he wish to avail of this opportunity to assist the Tribunal in its work, and repeated the requests for information contained in the letter of 27th March 1997. No reply was received to that letter.

On 1st May 1997 a letter was received from Mr. Charles Haughey personally which complained that he had not been put on notice of the Tribunal's intention to apply by letters of request to the English Court to have evidence taken there, and questioned the jurisdiction of the Senior Master in England to make the Order in favour of the Tribunal, and further alleged that the evidence being taken in London may not be admissible at the Tribunal.

On 15th May 1997 the Solicitor for the Tribunal again wrote to Mr. Charles Haughey requesting the information from him which had originally been sought on 27th March. Again no such information was furnished.

This was followed by a lengthy correspondence with Mr. Charles Haughey personally in which he questioned the Tribunal's procedures and the validity of Orders made by the Tribunal. On 20th June 1997 the Solicitor to the Tribunal wrote again looking for the information originally sought in the letter of 27th March. Again, no such information was furnished.

In the meantime, the Tribunal had furnished Mr. Charles Haughey with all witnesses statements and documents obtained by the Tribunal which related to him. Nevertheless, the lengthy correspondence continued without any information being given by Mr. Charles Haughey, and still apparently on the basis of his denial of the receipt of any monies contained in his letter of 7th March. It is not necessary in this Report to set out this entire correspondence in detail; it is sufficient to say that it was most unhelpful and very time consuming for the staff of the Tribunal to deal with.

On 30th June Mr. Charles Haughey was granted full representation and his Counsel stated that he would furnish a statement in which he would acknowledge that as a matter of probability £1.3 million pounds was paid into accounts managed by Mr. Desmond Traynor on his behalf but, he still denied that he had received the three bank drafts personally. The statement was furnished on 7th July, and is the statement set out in the Seventh Schedule hereto. On 9th July his Counsel read a further statement, being that set out in the Eighth Schedule to this report. In this statement Mr. Charles Haughey acknowledged that he had personally received the three bank drafts from Mr. Ben Dunne. When he gave evidence on 15th July he read yet another statement to the Tribunal, a copy of which is set out in the Ninth Schedule hereto. In his evidence on 15th July the question was put to Mr. Charles Haughey by Counsel for the Tribunal:—

> *"and would you accept now, Mr. Haughey, that you sat outside the Tribunal in Abbeville waiting to see whether or not the Tribunal would gather sufficient evidence to make it incumbent upon you to make a statement. Would that be a fair summation?"*

His reply was:—

> *"Well, it could be, but I suppose basically I was looking at the fact of the inevitable disclosure"*

He further conceded that it was not until the Tribunal had presented the evidence to him prior to 30th June 1997 that he decided to make a statement.

It is not for the Tribunal to determine whether Mr. Charles Haughey should be prosecuted pursuant to the section quoted above as this is a matter for the Director of Public Prosecutions. However, the Tribunal considers that the circumstances warrant the papers in the matter being sent to the Director of Public Prosecutions for his consideration as to whether there ought to be a prosecution, and the Tribunal intends to do so.

Chapter 11

Summary of Conclusions

Ordinary Political Donations

1. All payments considered under this heading were normal political contributions, and, other than that to the Wexford Branch of the Labour Party, were made by Mr. Ben Dunne on the basis of his personal regard for the individuals or organisations concerned, and were of amounts which he would have considered to be relatively small. The payment made to the Wexford Branch of the Labour Party was so small as to be insignificant. There was no further motive behind these payments.

Presidential Election

2. The cheque for £15,000 given by Mr. Ben Dunne to Mr. Ruairi Quinn was a spontaneous gesture on the part of Mr. Ben Dunne to contribute to Mrs. Mary Robinson's presidential campaign. The contribution was in fact used for that purpose.

3. This contribution was a personal contribution by Mr. Ben Dunne, and was not paid out of monies belonging to the Dunnes Stores Group. The motive for the payment was not to assist the Labour Party, but was to assist Mrs. Mary Robinson personally in her presidential campaign.

Waterworld plc

4. The payment of £50,000 given by Mr. Ben Dunne to Mr. Dick Spring was not intended to, nor did it, confer any benefit on Mr. Dick Spring or on the Labour Party. It was a normal transaction whereby the Dunnes Stores Group were, for commercial reasons, prepared to contribute to a facility in a town in which they did business.

The Fine Gael Party

5. Mr. Ben Dunne made three large contributions to the Fine Gael Party, amounting in all to £180,000. The payments were made following representations by senior members of the Fine Gael Party and appear to have

been made with the motive of assisting Fine Gael in its financial difficulties and of trying to ensure a stable opposition to the Government.

6. These payments were made out of the assets of the Dunnes Stores Group, but without the knowledge of the other directors or other shareholders in Dunnes Holding Company, and the final payment of £100,000 was paid in such a manner as to ensure confidentiality. There was no ulterior motive for the making of any of these payments.

Mr. Michael Lowry / Streamline Enterprises / Garuda Limited

7. The relationship between the Dunnes Stores Group on the one hand and Mr. Michael Lowry and Streamline Enterprises on the other hand was that Streamline Enterprises was responsible for the supply and maintenance of refrigeration equipment in all the Dunnes Stores outlets within the State. The terms of this agreement were never reduced to writing, and in financial terms, were vague in the extreme. The agreement was designed to put Streamline Enterprises into the position of being totally under the control of the Dunnes Stores Group so that it became virtually a division of the Dunnes Stores Group.

8. The financial aspect of this agreement was that Streamline Enterprises would be paid for their services in amounts which would allow them to show a small profit, while Mr. Michael Lowry would personally receive bonus payments. It was part of Mr. Ben Dunne's business philosophy that bonus payments were an important way of encouraging people and of getting a better performance out of people.

9. The relationship was extremely satisfactory from the point of view of the Dunnes Stores Group. Streamline Enterprises provided a skilled and efficient service resulting in very substantial savings to the Dunnes Stores Group.

10. In December of each year, between 1989 and 1992 inclusive, payments were made by Mr. Ben Dunne to Mr. Michael Lowry of amounts varying from £6,000 to £12,000 which were intended to be distributed by Mr. Michael Lowry as bonuses to the staff of Streamline Enterprises. Such bonuses were paid by Mr. Michael Lowry, although it is not possible to establish with certainty that the bonuses corresponded in total with the payments made.

11. Between November 1988 and March 1993 a number of cheques were issued by the Dunnes Stores Group in favour of Streamline Enterprises in relation to work carried out either in England or Northern Ireland. These cheques amounted in total to over £100,000 and were either cashed by Mr. Michael Lowry or lodged by him to accounts in his own name, and were not accounted for in the books and records of Streamline

Enterprises. Dunnes Stores Group at all times believed that these payments were being made to Streamline Enterprises and not to Mr. Michael Lowry personally.

12. Four sums amounting in all to £155,000 were paid by Mr. Ben Dunne to Mr. Michael Lowry between October 1990 and May 1992. These sums were intended to be bonus payments to Mr. Michael Lowry personally. Two of these payments were made into bank accounts in the Isle of Man, one in the name of Mr. Michael Lowry and the other in the name of Badgeworth Limited, which was a company that had been set up for the benefit of Mr. Michael Lowry on the instructions of Mr. Ben Dunne. These accounts were opened and the monies paid in this way with the intention of enabling Mr. Michael Lowry to have money in an off-shore account, contrary to the exchange control legislation then in being, and to assist him in evading tax.

13. Mr. Michael Lowry also had an account in the name of himself and his three children in the Jersey subsidiary of Allied Irish Banks, into which one of the cheques in an amount of £34,100 sterling paid to Streamline Enterprises in respect of work done in England was paid. This account was not opened with the assistance, or even with the knowledge of Mr. Ben Dunne, and again was an attempt by Mr. Michael Lowry to evade the payment of tax.

14. Dunnes Stores Group paid the sum of approximately £395,000 to contractors for refurbishment work done on the home of Mr. Michael Lowry at Holy Cross, Co. Tipperary. These payments were treated in the accounts of Dunnes Stores Group as having been payments for work done by the contractor for Dunnes Stores at the Ilac centre in Dublin and there is no record in the books of Dunnes Stores of these payments being made for the benefit of Mr. Michael Lowry. This method of payment was a very inefficient method of paying a bonus to Mr. Michael Lowry from the point of view of Dunnes Stores, and must have been made with a view to assisting him to evade tax.

15. The whole system whereby Mr. Michael Lowry would be paid substantial sums of money on a personal basis, and ultimately have a large sum of money spent on renovations to his house, were designed to, and did, assist him in evading tax.

16. The relationship between Dunnes Stores, Mr. Michael Lowry and Streamline Enterprises was an unhealthy business relationship under any circumstances, but was particularly disturbing in view of Mr. Michael Lowry's position as a public representative, and subsequently as Chairman of the Fine Gael Parliamentary Party and ultimately as a Cabinet Minister.

17. By evading tax in the way in which he did, Mr. Michael Lowry made himself vulnerable to all kinds of pressures from Dunnes Stores, had they chosen to apply those pressures. The threat to disclose the payments and

the off-shore accounts could have been used by Dunnes Stores to obtain favours, as indeed could a threat to cut off this source of income to Mr. Lowry.

18. Quite apart from potential pressure from Dunnes Stores, should the existence of these accounts have become known to any third party, such third party could seek either political or financial favours in return for silence.

19. It would be very damaging if there was a public perception that a person in the position of Government Minister and member of Cabinet was able to ignore with impunity, and indeed cynically evade, both taxation and exchange control laws of the State. It is an appalling situation that a Government Minister and Chairman of a Parliamentary Party can be seen to be consistently benefiting from the black economy from shortly after the time he was first elected to Dáil Éireann. If such a person can behave in this way without serious sanctions being imposed, it becomes very difficult to condemn others who similarly flout the law.

20. Neither Dunnes Stores nor Mr. Ben Dunne ever requested Mr. Michael Lowry to make any personal or political intervention on their behalf, and Mr. Michael Lowry never sought to intervene in any way for the benefit of Dunnes Stores or Mr. Ben Dunne. There was no political impropriety on the part of Mr. Michael Lowry.

Mr. Charles Haughey

21. Mr. Ben Dunne made four payments for the benefit of Mr. Charles Haughey amounting in all to some £1.1 million at the request of Mr. Desmond Traynor, which request was transmitted through Mr. Noel Fox.

22. In addition, Mr. Ben Dunne personally handed three bank drafts for £70,000 sterling each to Mr. Charles Haughey in November 1991 as a spontaneous gesture, and without any request for funds having been made to him.

23. All of the initial £1.1 million was ultimately paid through Mr. Desmond Traynor into an account of a Cayman Islands bank known as Ansbacher Cayman Limited with Guinness & Mahon (Ireland) Limited in Dublin, having been routed through various accounts in England. The three bank drafts constituting the final payment of £210,000 sterling were lodged by Mr. Desmond Traynor directly to an account of Ansbacher Cayman Limited with Irish Intercontinental Bank in Dublin.

24. The first payment of £182,630 sterling was transferred from the account of Ansbacher Cayman Limited to an account of Amiens Investments Limited with Guinness & Mahon (Ireland) Limited. Amiens Investments Limited was a company owned and controlled by Mr. Desmond Traynor, and this money was then disbursed for the benefit of Mr. Charles Haughey by

Amiens Investments Limited, including a payment of £105,000 to Agricultural Credit Corporation to discharge a debt owing by Mr. Charles Haughey to that organisation.

25. Mr. Desmond Traynor was Chairman of Ansbacher Cayman Limited, which had originally been a subsidiary of Guinness & Mahon (Ireland) Limited at a time when Mr. Desmond Traynor was Deputy Chairman and in effect chief executive of Guinness & Mahon (Ireland) Limited. He acted on behalf of a number of Irish persons who wished to deposit their money off-shore, and deposited the money on their behalf in Ansbacher Cayman Limited. At the same time Ansbacher Cayman Limited deposited the monies which it had received from Irish clients in its own name with Guinness & Mahon (Ireland) Limited. It is not known whether each Irish client had a separate deposit account with Ansbacher Cayman Limited, as it has not been possible to obtain access to the records of that bank, but some form of internal accounting or memorandum accounts exists accounting for the funds of each Irish client.

26. During his lifetime Mr. Desmond Traynor controlled monies deposited in this manner on behalf of Mr. Charles Haughey with Ansbacher Cayman Limited. Each of the last four payments made by Mr. Ben Dunne, namely the payments of £471,000 sterling, £150,000 sterling, £200,000 sterling and £210,000 sterling, were paid into accounts in the name of Ansbacher Cayman Limited and formed part of the monies deposited by Ansbacher Cayman Limited with Guinness & Mahon (Ireland) Limited and Irish Intercontinental Bank. At least two of the memorandum accounts or sub-accounts in Ansbacher Cayman Limited were held for the benefit of Mr. Charles Haughey, being those designated S8 and S9.

27. After the death of Mr. Desmond Traynor, the monies held on behalf of Mr. Charles Haughey came under the control of Mr. John Furze, who was a joint managing director of Ansbacher Cayman Limited. In about the year 1992 some of these monies were transferred into an account of Hamilton Ross Co. Limited, a company owned and controlled by Mr. John Furze, with Irish Intercontinental Bank.

28. For many years prior to 1991 Mr. Charles Haughey's day to day financial affairs were dealt with by his former accountancy firm of Haughey Boland, which paid all his personal and household expenses. It received the necessary funds to pay his expenses from Mr. Desmond Traynor during his lifetime, and after his death from Mr. Padraig Collery. Such funds were withdrawn by Mr. Desmond Traynor or Mr. Padraig Collery initially from the account of Ansbacher Cayman Limited with Guinness & Mahon (Ireland) Limited and Irish Intercontinental Bank and subsequently from the account of Hamilton Ross Co. Limited with Irish Intercontinental Bank.

29. It has been shown without doubt that the last four payments by Mr. Ben Dunne for the benefit of Mr. Charles Haughey were paid into accounts in the name of Ansbacher Cayman Limited with Guinness & Mahon (Ireland) Limited and Irish Intercontinental Bank, and it has been shown that substantial payments for the benefit of Mr. Charles Haughey were paid out of such accounts. Beyond this, it is not possible to establish whether the payments by Mr. Ben Dunne were used solely to discharge Mr. Charles Haughey's living and household expenses, or whether such payments may have been used to discharge other substantial debts of Mr. Charles Haughey. Such information could only come from the detailed memorandum accounts or the internal documents of Ansbacher Cayman Limited.

30. Mr. Desmond Traynor and Mr. Padraig Collery kept detailed records of the accounts of the Irish customers of Ansbacher Cayman Limited, including Mr. Charles Haughey. However, shortly after the death of Mr. Desmond Traynor a number of such records were destroyed or taken back to the Cayman Islands by Mr. John Furze, and Mr. Padraig Collery has given evidence that he no longer has any records relating to the affairs of Mr. Charles Haughey. It is probable that such records do exist, either in the files of Ansbacher Cayman Limited or in documents held by the late Mr. John Furze at the time of his death.

31. Mr. Ciaran Haughey is a son of Mr. Charles Haughey and is a director of and substantial shareholder in Celtic Helicopters Limited. His firm did a considerable amount of work for the Dunnes Stores Group, and for Mr. Ben Dunne personally, and in October 1988 Mr. Ben Dunne gave Mr. Ciaran Haughey a cheque for £10,000, which was in the nature of a bonus payment to Mr. Ciaran Haughey personally.

32. On four occasions funds held for the benefit of Mr. Charles Haughey and forming part of the deposits of Ansbacher Cayman Limited with Guinness & Mahon (Ireland) Limited and Irish Intercontinental Bank were used to support debts of Celtic Helicopters Limited. In February 1992 a loan from Irish Intercontinental Bank to Celtic Helicopters Limited of £150,000 was repaid out of the Ansbacher Cayman Limited general deposit account with Irish Intercontinental Bank, from monies held on behalf of Mr. Charles Haughey. While it is possible that Mr. Ciaran Haughey was not aware of the monies being used to support the loans to the company, he must have been aware of the repayment of the £150,000 loan.

33. The Tribunal has been unable to accept much of the evidence of Mr. Charles Haughey. In particular, the Tribunal cannot accept Mr. Charles Haughey's assertion that he was at no time aware that monies were held for his benefit in Ansbacher Cayman Limited and the Tribunal believes that he must have become aware of the existence of these monies shortly after the death of Mr. Desmond Traynor at the very latest. The Tribunal

also cannot believe that Mr. Charles Haughey was not aware of the taxation implications of the receipt of gifts of this magnitude from Mr. Ben Dunne, but rather believes that Mr. Charles Haughey deliberately shrouded the gifts in secrecy and allowed the money to be kept off-shore in an attempt to ensure that the Revenue authorities would never know of the gifts, or indeed presumably of the existence of interest paid on the monies deposited on his behalf.

34. It is quite unacceptable that a member of Dáil Éireann, and in particular a Cabinet Minister and Taoiseach, should be supported in his personal lifestyle by gifts made to him personally. It is particularly unacceptable that such gifts should emanate from prominent businessmen within the State. The possibility that political or financial favours could be sought in return for such gifts, or even be given without being sought, is very high, and if such gifts are permissible, they would inevitably lead in some cases to bribery and corruption.

35. It is also not acceptable that any person or commercial enterprise should make such gifts in conditions of secrecy, no matter how well intentioned the motives may have been.

36. There is no evidence of any favours sought of Mr. Charles Haughey by Mr. Ben Dunne, the Dunne family or the Dunnes Stores Group, nor is there any evidence of any attempt by Mr. Charles Haughey to exercise his influence for the benefit of Mr. Ben Dunne, the Dunne family or the Dunnes Stores Group. There appears in fact to have been no political impropriety on the part of Mr. Charles Haughey in relation to these gifts but that does not take away from the unacceptable nature of them.

37. The large majority of the payments made by Mr. Ben Dunne which have been considered in this report were made without the knowledge or approval of the Board of Directors of Dunnes Holding Company and without the knowledge or approval of his co-shareholders in that company, although such payments were made out of funds which were the property of one or more companies in the Dunnes Stores Group. It was clearly unwise that one person should be given such unsupervised financial control of the affairs of a business the size of the Dunnes Stores Group, and as a matter of general principle the company must have some responsibility for the actions of an officer to whom it delegates such wide powers.

38. The attitude of Mr. Charles Haughey in relation to the Tribunal has been such as might amount to an offence under section 1(2) of the Tribunals of Inquiry (Evidence) Act 1921 as amended by the Tribunals of Inquiry (Evidence) (Amendment) Act 1979. All relevant papers will be sent to the Director of Public Prosecutions for his consideration and decision as to whether Mr. Charles Haughey should be prosecuted under this section.

Chapter 12

Recommendations

The combined effect of the Ethics in Public Office Act 1995 and the Electoral Act 1997 amounts to a commendable attempt to ensure that the unacceptable elements of the financial transactions of which Mr. Michael Lowry and Mr. Charles Haughey were part will not be repeated. However, as many of the payments to Mr. Michael Lowry and Mr. Charles Haughey were made off-shore and in a manner veiled in secrecy in an attempt to ensure that they would remain undiscovered, it may be that the measures in the recent legislation do not go far enough. If a member of either House of the Oireachtas is going to become involved in such operations, then that member will almost certainly not comply with his or her obligations to register the payments. A person who goes to such lengths to deceive the Revenue Authorities and the public will almost certainly go to equal lengths to deceive the Oireachtas. It is, of course, impossible to ensure that gifts will not be made secretly to members of the Oireachtas, and the Tribunal can only recommend that there should be greater sanctions for any breach of the obligations imposed by the Ethics in Public Office Act. Having said that, the Tribunal welcomes the recent legislation, and considers in particular that it should be highly effective in monitoring ordinary political donations.

The Tribunal has considered with interest the proposals put forward by the Fianna Fáil Party in its submissions. On balance, the Tribunal does not consider it practical, or indeed that it would be particularly effective, to oblige bankers, accountants or other professional advisers to disclose any unusual or large financial transactions involving politicians or public servants. The reality is that if there was such an obligation, it could only be imposed on advisers within the State, and such provisions could be easily avoided by the politician or public servant concerned simply acting through advisers and banks outside the State.

The question of an independent third party appointed by the Oireachtas to monitor and investigate possible breaches of the Ethics in Public Office Act is an interesting one. While the Tribunal does not consider that there would be sufficient justification for setting up a totally new office, it does feel that consideration should be given to extending the jurisdiction of the Ombudsman to include these functions. This might involve extending his powers to enable him to carry out investigations by the making of certain forms of orders, such as orders for discovery of documents, and possibly by allowing him to have recourse to the Courts to seek letters of requests to Courts in other jursidictions to enable witnesses to be examined or documents to be produced in such jurisdictions. This Tribunal has found those powers to be extremely beneficial in its investigations.

The Tribunal does consider that it should be mandatory for any candidate for either House of the Oireachtas to produce to the Clerk of the Dáil or the Seanad, as the case may be, a certificate from such person's tax inspector that his or her tax affairs are in order, and this should be accompanied by a statutory declaration from the person concerned to that effect.

The Tribunal believes that sanctions for failure to make disclosures should be strengthened in two ways. Firstly, the making of a false declaration of interest should be a criminal offence, and not merely dealt with internally by the House of the Oireachtas concerned. Secondly, consideration should be given to some form of legislation which would provide that any person found guilty of an offence under the Ethics in Public Office Act would be ineligible to become a member of either House in the future, either for a limited period or permanently.

Finally, although it may be somewhat outside the terms of reference, the Tribunal has given some consideration to the general position of the funding of politicians and political parties. The Tribunal does not consider it practical to prohibit all political contributions and rely solely on public funding of political parties. Indeed, to do so might give rise to serious constitutional difficulties. Even the system of disclosure set up under the Ethics in Public Office Act 1995 is open to abuse, but if the stronger sanctions suggested above are put in place, it is probably neither necessary nor desirable to restrict further the system of political donations, at least until the provisions of that Act have been given a reasonable period to prove themselves.

The Honourable Mr. Justice Brian McCracken

SCHEDULES

First Schedule

Tribunals of Inquiry (Evidence) Acts, 1921 and 1979, Order, 1997

Tribunals of Inquiry (Evidence) Acts, 1921 and 1979, Order, 1997:

WHEREAS a Resolution in the following terms was passed by Dáil Éireann and by Seanad Éireann on the 6th day of February, 1997.

"Bearing in mind serious public concern about alleged payments made and benefits conferred by, or on behalf of, Dunnes Holding Company, other associated companies or entities and/or companies or trusts controlled directly or indirectly by members of the Dunne Family between 1st January, 1986 and 31st December, 1996, to persons who were members of the Houses of the Oireachtas during that period or relatives or connected persons as defined in the Ethics in Public Office Act, 1995, to political parties, or to other public representatives or other public servants,

And noting the Interim Report of the Independent Person appointed pursuant to an Agreement dated the 9th day of December, 1996, made between the Government and Dunnes Holding Company,

Resolves that it is expedient that a Tribunal be established, under the Tribunals of Inquiry (Evidence) Act, 1921, as adapted by or under subsequent enactments, and the Tribunals of Inquiry (Evidence) (Amendment) Act, 1979, to enquire urgently into, and report to the Clerk of the Dáil and make such findings and recommendations as it sees fit, in relation to the following definite matters of urgent public importance:

(a) all payments in cash or in kind directly or indirectly whether authorised or unauthorised within or without the State which were made to or received by

   (i) persons who were between 1st January, 1986 and 31st December, 1996, members of the Houses of the Oireachtas,

   (ii) their relatives or connected persons as defined in the Ethics in Public Office Act, 1995,

   (iii) political parties

from Dunnes Holding Company and/or any associated enterprises as defined in the Schedule hereto and/or Mr. Ben Dunne or any person on his behalf or any companies, trusts or other entities controlled directly or indirectly by Mr. Ben Dunne between 1st January, 1986, and 31st December, 1996, and the considerations, motives and circumstances therefor;

(b) Such further matters as Dáil Éireann and Seanad Éireann might by further Resolution consider appropriate to refer to the Tribunal because they require further investigation, relating to other payments made to "Relevant Persons or Entities" within the meaning of the Agreement dated 9th day of December, 1996, made between the Government and Dunnes Holding Company, following receipt by the Ceann Comhairle and the Cathaoirleach of Seanad Éireann of any further report from the Independent Person appointed pursuant to the said Agreement whereupon such report shall be laid before both Houses of the Oireachtas immediately on its receipt.

And that the Tribunal be asked to report, on an interim basis, not later than the tenth day of any oral hearing to the Clerk of the Dáil on the following matters:

the number of parties then represented before the Tribunal;

the progress which has been made in the hearing and the work of the Tribunal;

the likely duration (so far as that may be capable of being estimated at that point in time) of the Tribunal proceedings;

any other matters which the Tribunal believes should be drawn to the attention of the Clerk of the Dáil at that stage (including any matter relating to the terms of reference);

And that the persons selected to conduct the Inquiry should be informed that it is the desire of the House that the Inquiry be completed in as economical a manner as possible, and at the earliest date consistent with a fair examination of the matters referred to it;

And that the Clerk of the Dáil shall on receipt of any Report from the Tribunal arrange to have it laid before both Houses of the Oireachtas immediately on its receipt.

SCHEDULE

Associated enterprises shall include:

(1) Ben Lettery Limited, Green Arch Corporation, Dunnes Stores Limited (which with Dunnes Holding Company shall hereafter be referred to as "the Dunne Companies")

(2) Any company inside or outside the State of which any of the Dunne Companies were during the relevant period a subsidiary within the meaning of section 155 of the Companies Act, 1963

(3) Any subsidiary of any of the Dunne Companies within the meaning of section 155 of the Companies Act, 1963, either inside or outside the State

(4) Any director or shadow director (as defined by section 27 of the Companies Act, 1990, of any of the companies referred to at 2) or 3) above)

(5) Any company or other body or entity inside or outside the State which directly or indirectly within the relevant period was under the control of any of the Dunne Companies or any of the Directors thereof (whether alone or with any other person) or in respect of which the Directors of any of the Dunne Companies were either directors or shadow directors within the meaning of section 27 of the Companies Act, 1990, or any company or other body or entity inside or outside the State whose directors, officers or employees were accustomed to act and did act on the direction or control of any of the Dunne Companies or the Directors or any of them within the relevant period

(6) Any company, other body or other entity inside or outside the State over whose operations or financial policy any of the Dunne Companies, their directors or any of them exercised a significant influence within the relevant period

(7) Any trust company inside or outside the State which acted during the relevant period under the direction or control of any of the Dunne Companies or any of their directors or any trust inside or outside the State in respect of which any of the Dunne Companies or any of the Directors or any relatives or connected persons of such Directors either alone or with any person were beneficiaries within the relevant period

(8) Any other company, body, trust or entity inside or outside the State controlled by Mr. Ben Dunne or any of his relatives within the meaning of the Ethics in Public Office Act, 1995, whether alone or with any other person or in respect of which any of the said persons, their or any of their relatives or any persons connected to them or any of them were beneficial owners or beneficiaries"

NOW I, John Bruton, Taoiseach, in pursuance of those Resolutions, and in exercise of the powers conferred on me by section 1 (as adapted by or under subsequent enactments) of the Tribunals of Inquiry (Evidence) Act, 1921, hereby order as follows:

1. This Order may be cited as the Tribunals of Inquiry (Evidence) Acts, 1921 and 1979, Order, 1997.

2. A Tribunal is hereby appointed to enquire urgently into and report and make such findings and recommendations as it sees fit to the Clerk of the Dáil on the definite matters of urgent public importance set out at paragraphs (a) and (b) of the Resolutions passed by Dáil Éireann and Seanad Éireann on the 6th day of February, 1997.

3. The Honourable Mr. Justice Brian McCracken, a Judge of the High Court, is hereby nominated to be the sole member of the Tribunal.

4. The Tribunals of Inquiry (Evidence) Act, 1921 (as adapted by or under subsequent enactments) and the Tribunals of Inquiry (Evidence) (Amendment) Act, 1979, shall apply to the Tribunal.

GIVEN under my Official Seal, this
7th day of February, 1997

John Bruton
TAOISEACH

Second Schedule

Extracts from Particulars Arising out of Mr. Ben Dunne's Legal Proceedings

---

Noel Smyth & Partners

Solicitors
Commissioners for Oaths

22 Fitzwilliam Square,
Dublin 2.
Tel: (01) 661 5525 / 661 3981
D.D.E. 34,
Fax No. 661 3979,
Vat No. IE F4645234J

Noel M. Smyth
Ronan Hannigan
T. Colman Bermingham
Gerard O'Shea

Our Ref: Your Ref.   Date
    NS/pf   November 4, 1994

STRICTLY PRIVATE & CONFIDENTIAL
ADDRESSEE ONLY:
Boyce Shubotham Esq.,
Messrs, William Fry,
Solicitors,
Fitzwilton House,
Wilton Place,
Dublin 2.

Re: Ben Dunne-v-Noel Fox, Edward Montgomery, Frank Bowen,
Bernard Uniacke
The High Court 1993 Record No. 7722P

Dear Sir,

We refer to your letter of the 28th of October in regard to the furnishing of Particulars sought by you in your letter of the 12th of October.

We have already made our position quite clear in our letter of the 14th of October. That letter sets out in details why you are not entitled to the Particulars sought. You have failed to address in a substantive way our objections to Replying Particulars, which we believe are well founded.

In the light of the Motion we have reviewed the position. We are quite satisfied that our position is a correct and proper one, and that the Notice for Particulars is vexatious. Our views on this regard have been confirmed by an examination of the Price Waterhouse Discovery.

Notwithstanding our position as set out above, we do acknowledge the importance which our Client's allegation, that the Trustees facilitated the making of payments to third parties, has for our attack on the validity of the Trust and the 1985 Appointment. While we still believe that we are correct in saying that it is the fact of the payments, rather than the details of each payment that is relevant, we are prepared, without prejudice to our position, to give you details of those payments on which we rely. We enclose those details in the Schedule attached to this letter.

We wish to make it quite clear that the above concession should not be misinterpreted. We intend resisting your Motion next Monday, and we will demonstrate to the Court by reliance on the Affidavits sworn by us in connection with our Client's Motion as to why we believe the Application to be vexatious.

Yours faithfully,

Noel Smyth
_____
NOEL SMYTH

NOEL SMYTH & PARTNERS

SCHEDULE OF PAYMENTS

Referred to in the letter of 4th November, 1994
Noel Smyth & Partners — William Fry

	Recipient	Amount	Defendants involved in or with Knowledge of Payment.
1.	C. J. Haughey	£1 Million +	Noel Fox, Frank Bowen, Frank Dunne, Margaret Heffernan.

	Recipient	Amount	Defendants involved in or with Knowledge of Payment.
3.	Fine Gael	£200K	Noel Fox.

THE HIGH COURT

BETWEEN:

BERNARD DUNNE

Plaintiff

— and —

NOEL FOX, EDWARD MONTGOMERY,
FRANK BOWEN, BERNARD UNIACKE,
and by Order of the Court FRANK DUNNE,
MARGARET HEFFERNAN AND THERESE DUNNE
and by further Order of the Court
LESLIE MELLON and JOHN O'DONOVAN

Defendants

NOTICE FOR PARTICULARS

WILLIAM FRY
Solicitors
Fitzwilton House
Wilton Place
Dublin 2
Ref: 11418-014-BS

86

THE HIGH COURT

BETWEEN:

BERNARD DUNNE

Plaintiff

— and —

NOEL FOX, EDWARD MONTGOMERY,
FRANK BOWEN, BERNARD UNIACKE,
and by Order of the Court FRANK DUNNE,
and by further Order of the Court
LESLIE MELLON and JOHN O'DONOVAN

Defendants

NOTICE FOR PARTICULARS

TAKE NOTICE that the fifth, sixth and seventh named Defendants require further particulars of the following matters which the plaintiff, by letter dated 4 November 1994 has stated he relies upon in this action;

1. C. J. Haughey — £1m+

    (a) the amount or amounts alleged to have been paid to C. J. Haughey;

    (b) when the amount or amounts were paid;

    (c) how the amount and/or amounts were paid;

    (d) if the payment was other than by cash, particulars of the bank account/accounts from which the payment/payments were made and to which the payment/payments were made;

    (e) the party/parties who directed the payment/payments to be made;

    (f) if the party who directed the payment differs from the party/parties who executed any banking documentation to effect payment details of the latter parties;

    (g) in the event of any payment being made in a manner that was not directly to C. J. Haughey particulars of the person or persons, corporation or other legal entity or nominee to whom the payments were made;

    (h) the basis upon which it is alleged Margaret Heffernan knew and/or was involved in the making of such payment;

    (i) the basis upon which it is alleged Frank Dunne knew and/or was involved in the making of such payment;

2. Fine Gael — £200K

    (a) when the said sum was paid;

    (b) how the said sum was paid;

    (c) if the payment was other than if by cash particulars of the bank account/accounts from which the payment/payments were made and the bank accounts to which the payment/payments were made;

    (d) the party/parties who directed the payment/payments be made;

    (e) if the party who directed the payments differs from the party/parties who executed any banking documentation to effect payment details of the latter parties;

Dated this 7 day of November 1994

Signed: ....
        William Fry
        Solicitors for the fifth, sixth & seventh named Defendants
        Fitzwilton House,
        Wilton Place,
        Dublin 2.

To: Noel Smyth & Partners
        Solicitors
        22 Fitzwilliam Square
        Dublin 2

BETWEEN:—

BERNARD DUNNE

Plaintiff

— and —

NOEL FOX, EDWARD MONTGOMERY, FRANK BOWEN
AND BERNARD UNIACKE

AND BY ORDER OF THE COURT

FRANK DUNNE, MARGARET HEFFERNAN AND THERESE DUNNE

AND BY FURTHER ORDER OF THE COURT

LESLIE MELLON AND JOHN O'DONOVAN

Defendants

REPLY TO NOTICE FOR PARTICULARS

TAKE NOTICE that the Plaintiff delivers the following Replies to the Notice for Particulars served herein on the 7th November, 1994.

1. C. J. Haughey — £1m+

 (a) (i) STG£471,000.00 (Irish equivalent at that time £500,000.00);

 (ii) STG£250,000.00;

 (iii) STG£150,000.00; and finally

 (iv) STG£200,000.00.

 (b) (i) 14th July, 1988;

 (ii) between 1988 and 1989;

 (iii) 3rd May, 1989;

 (iv) between 1990 and 1991;

 (c) (i) the payment of STG£471,000.00:—

 This amount was paid by way of a transfer of STG£471,000.00 from a US$ deposit account maintained Equifex Trust Corporation AG — Tse Kam Ming, maintained at Zug, Switzerland. The money was transferred to a client account in the name of Froriep Renggli & Partners, and from thence to Barclays Bank plc, 68, Knightsbridge, London SW1X 7LW for credit to account number 40384976 in the name of John A. Furze.

(ii) Payment from Dunnes Stores (Bangor) Limited by means of a cheque made payable to John A. Furze. No further details available.

(iii) STG£150,000.00 by telegraphic transfer to Royal Bank of Scotland, 62/63, Threadneedle Street, London, EC3.

Sort Code: 16-00-05.

Account Henry Ansbacher & Co. Limited.

Account Number: 11215626.

For further credit to account number 190017/202 through Equifex Corporation AG — Tse Kam Ming US$ account on the directions of Marcus Stadler Esquire, Froriep Renggli & Partners, 6300 Zug., Baarerstr 75, Switzerland.

(iv) STG£200,000.00 from Rea Bros. (IOM) Limited of Georges Street, Douglas, Isle of Man by telex transfer. Further details are not available. The receiving Bank however was Henry Ansbacher & Co. Limited in London.

(d) The payments were in cash, the details of which are referred to above.

(e) The Plaintiff in the case of payments (i), (ii), (iii) and (iv) directed the payments to be made. In the case of (ii), the Plaintiff directed the first named Defendant to make the payment who in turn instructed the Executive Directors Dunnes Stores (Bangor) Limited to make the payment.

(f) In respect of number (i) and (iii), the details are the same, namely Marcus Stadler. In respect of number (ii) the payment was made at the direction of the Plaintiff and the cheque executed by Directors of Dunnes Stores (Bangor) Limited. In the case of number (iv) the payment was made at the direction of the Plaintiff but the details of the banking officers who carried out the transaction are not available.

(g) Details of the payments and by whom they were effected are more particularly set out at (a) to (f) above.

(h) Margaret Heffernan knew ex post facto of the payments having been made but was not involved in the making of such payments.

2. Fine Gael — £200K

(a) The sums were paid over a period of two to three years from 1989 to 1992.

(b) The said sums were paid by cheques.

(c) The payments would have been made from the bank account at Bank of Ireland, Marino, Ben Dunne T/A as Dunnes Stores at the direction of the Plaintiff.

(d) As (c) above.

(e) No, see (c) above.

Dated this   day of   , 1994.

_____

Noel Smyth & Partners
Solicitors
22 Fitzwilliam Square
Dublin 2

To: William Fry
Solicitors,
Fitzwilton House,
Wilton Place,
Dublin 2.

Third Schedule

Memorandum on Confidentiality

Tribunal of Inquiry
(Dunnes Payments)

Memorandum Re: Documentation

This Memorandum sets out the basic procedures which the Tribunal intends to adopt in relation to documentation which is submitted to it in the course of its work. It is not intended to be a legally binding document and there may be circumstances in which, in relation to one or more documents, a different course might be adopted than that outlined below. The treatment of documents submitted to the Tribunal shall be subject to the overriding discretion of the Sole Member of the Tribunal, whose decision shall be final.

1. The Tribunal recognises that parties who submit documents, or who may be referred to, or whose affairs may be referred to, in documents submitted by other parties, have a legitimate interest in ensuring that confidential or sensitive information, whether of a commercial or other nature, which is not relevant, is not made public or available for public scrutiny either now or any time in the future. At all times the Tribunal will strive to ensure as far as reasonably practicable and consistent with the task which has been imposed on the Tribunal, to ensure that the aforesaid legitimate interest of parties is respected.

2. Documents which are submitted to the Tribunal will be kept in Dublin Castle under conditions of strict security. Such documents will be available in the first instance only to the Sole Member of the Tribunal, Counsel acting for the Tribunal, the Solicitor acting for the Tribunal, the Registrar to the Tribunal and the Tribunal's office manager. Security procedures in relation to the documentation will be supervised and implemented by the Tribunal's office manager.

3. The Tribunal recognises that in some cases, only part of a document submitted will be relevant to the Tribunal's inquiries and that the balance of such document may be irrelevant, while none the less containing information which may be commercially sensitive or otherwise private. In so far as any use is made by the Tribunal of such documents, it is the Tribunal's intention to block out all irrelevant commercially sensitive or

otherwise private material in such documentation. The witness or person who is given or shown such document will only be shown a copy with all such portions blocked out.

4. It may not always be the case that those portions of the documents which are relevant and those portions which are irrelevant will be immediately apparent. The Tribunal proposes to retain the entire document until it is satisfied that it is in a position to correctly identify and distinguish the relevant and irrelevant portions of the document. It is however, the Tribunal's intention to return originals and full copies to the party or parties who may have submitted such documents once the Tribunal is satisfied it has identified the relevant part of such documents. In such cases, the Tribunal will retain copies with such irrelevant portions blocked out. The Tribunal reserves the power to direct any party to whom it has returned a full copy or original document to give such full copy or original document back to the Tribunal.

5. Counsel for the Tribunal will at all times be willing to discuss which portions of a document, if any, should be blocked out as containing irrelevant material. While the decision on relevance or irrelevance must ultimately remain a matter for the Tribunal and its Counsel, the Tribunal and its Counsel will seek to accommodate and respect every concern which may be expressed by a party in relation to irrelevant material in a document.

6. After the Tribunal has made its final report, it will intend to return all original documents and destroy all copies, but the Tribunal reserves the right to retain such documentation for such a period as the Tribunal may think fit, having regard to the risk of any litigation which might arise involving the Tribunal. All such documents will be securely retained and, in due course returned or destroyed.

Fourth Schedule

List of parties ordered to give evidence before the Tribunal in London

1. David Morgan, Barclays Bank plc, Lombard Street

2. David Vugler, Barclays Bank plc, Lombard Street

3. Peter Hinson, Barclays Bank plc, Knightsbridge

4. Paul Gatward, Barclays Bank plc, Knightsbridge

5. Morag Vaughan, Royal Bank of Scotland

6. Rose Brownlie, Royal Bank of Scotland

7. Hamish Graham Hershel Ramsay, Henry Ansbacher & Co.

8. Peter Greenhalgh, Henry Ansbacher & Co.

9. Caroline Susan Freeman, Guinness Mahon & Co.

10. Kevin Downey, Guinness Mahon & Co.

11. David Green, Guinness Mahon & Co.

Fifth Schedule

List of parties whose evidence was sought in the Cayman Islands

---

1. Managers or proper officers of Ansbacher (Cayman) Limited, of Ansbacher House, George Town, Grand Cayman.

2. John A. Furze c/o Myers & Alberga, Attorneys at Law, Midland Bank Building, George Town, Grand Cayman.

3. John A. Collins of Ansbacher (Cayman) Limited, Ansbacher House, George Town, Grand Cayman.

4. Hugh Hart of Ansbacher (Cayman) Limited, Ansbacher House, George Town, Grand Cayman.

5. Michael Day of Ansbacher (Cayman) Limited, Ansbacher House, George Town, Grand Cayman.

6. H. Kervin Glidden of Ansbacher (Cayman) Limited, Ansbacher House, George Town, Grand Cayman.

7. J. Maxine Everson, of Ansbacher (Cayman) Limited, Ansbacher House, George Town, Grand Cayman.

8. Bryan Bothwell, of Ansbacher (Cayman) Limited, Ansbacher House, George Town, Grand Cayman.

9. The audit partners of KPMG (Cayman), Genises Building, George Town, Grand Cayman.

Sixth Schedule

List of witnesses who appeared before the Tribunal

PART I

Monday 21st April 1997

  Mr Ben Dunne

Tuesday 22nd April 1997

Mr Ben Dunne	— Former Chairman and Executive Director of Dunnes Holding Company
Mr Noel Fox	— Chartered Accountant, Senior Partner in Oliver Freaney & Company, joint auditor of Dunnes Stores Group, one of the Trustees of the Dunnes Settlement Trust

Wednesday 23rd April 1997

Mr Matthew Price	— Director of Dunnes Stores (Bangor) Limited
Mr Michael Irwin	— Chartered Accountant, former Chief Accountant of Dunnes Stores Group
Ms Pauline Finnerty	— Secretary and Personal Assistant to Noel Smyth, Solicitor of Noel Smyth & Partners
Mr Colm Hilliard	— former TD for the Meath Constituency

Thursday 24th April 1997

Mr Dick Spring TD	— TD for the Constituency of North Kerry, the then Tánaiste and Minister for Foreign Affairs
Mr Brian Durran	— Secretary of Tralee Waterworld plc and Tralee Partnership and Enterprise Company Limited
Mr Albert Dudgeon	— Banker with Rea Brothers (Isle of Man) Limited

Mr Julian Harper	— Director of ECS International Limited, Isle of Man
Mr Pat Farrell	— General Secretary of Fianna Fail Party
Mr Jim Miley	— General Secretary of Fine Gael Party
Mr Ray Kavanagh	— General Secretary of the Labour Party
Mr Ruairi Quinn TD	— TD for Dublin South-East, the then Minister for Finance

Friday 25th April 1997

Mrs Margaret Heffernan	— Director of Dunnes Holding Company
Mr Noel Smyth	— Principal of Noel Smyth & Partners, Solicitors and Solicitor acting for Ben Dunne

Monday 28th April 1997

Mr John Bruton TD	— TD for the County of Meath, Leader of Fine Gael Party and the then Taoiseach
Mr Sean Haughey TD	— TD for Dublin North-Central; son of Charles J. Haughey
Mr Alan Dukes TD	— TD for County Kildare; the then Minister for Transport, Energy & Communications
Mr Michael Noonan TD	— TD for Limerick East; the then Minister for Health
Mr Ivan Yates TD	— TD for County Wexford; the then Minister for Agriculture, Food & Forestry
Mr Sean Barrett TD	— TD for Dún Laoghaire; the then Minister for Defence and the Marine
Mr Jim Mitchell TD	— TD for Dublin Central
Mr Fintan Coogan	— Former TD for Galway
Mr Peter Stevens	— Principal Architect with Peter Stevens & Associates
Mr Jack Tierney	— Managing Director of Faxhill Homes Limited

PART II

Wednesday 2nd July 1997

Mr Ivan Doherty — General Secretary of Fine Gael Party from 1990 — 1995

Mr Bernard Walsh — Manager with Dunnes Stores

Mr Michael Miley — Programme Manager to Ivan Yates, when he was Minister for Agriculture, Food & Forestry

Mr Mark Kennelly — Special Advisor to Michael Lowry when he was Minister for Transport, Energy & Communications

Mr Phil Hogan TD — TD for the constituency of Carlow-Kilkenny, current Chairman for Fine Gael Party

Mr Paul McGrath TD — TD for Co Westmeath

Mr Ben Dunne

Mr Michael Lowry TD — TD for Tipperary North and former Minister for Transport, Energy & Communications

Thursday 3rd July 1997

Mr Michael Lowry

Friday 4th July 1997

Mr Michael Lowry

Wednesday 9th July 1997

Mr Noel Smyth

Thursday 10th July 1997

Ms Sandra Kells — Finance Director of Guinness & Mahon (Ireland) Limited

Mr John Hickey — former Deputy Chief Executive of Agricultural Credit Corporation, now retired

Mr Tony Barnes — Associate Director with Irish Intercontinental Bank

Mr John Reynolds — Director of Irish Intercontinental Bank

Friday 11th July 1997

    Mr Paul Carty — Chartered Accountant, Managing Partner of Deloitte & Touche

    Mr Padraig Collery — former banker with Guinness & Mahon (Ireland) Limited, now with Kindle Computer Banking Systems

    Mr Jack Stakelum — Chartered Accountant, Financial Consultant with Business Enterprises Limited

    Mr Cathal MacDomhnaill — current Chairman of Revenue Commissioners

    Mr Philip Curran — former Chairman of Revenue Commissioners

    Mr Noel Smyth, Solicitor

Monday 14th July 1997

    Mr Noel Smyth

    Mr Bernard Uniacke — Chartered Accountant; one of the Trustees of the Dunnes Settlement Trust

    Mr Ben Dunne

    Mr Ciaran Haughey — helicopter pilot and Director of Celtic Helicopters, son of Charles J. Haughey

    Mr Jimmy Farrelly — Secretary to the Department of the Environment

    Mr Dermot Smyth — Assistant Secretary to the Department of Health

Tuesday 15th July 1997

    Mr Charles J. Haughey — Former Taoiseach

Seventh Schedule

Copy statement of Charles J. Haughey dated 15th July 1997

Tribunal of Inquiry
(Dunnes Payments)

Appointed by Instrument of an Taoiseach
Dated 7th February 1997

Sole Member the Honourable Mr Justice Brian McCracken

<u>**Statement of Charles J. Haughey**</u>

(Furnished by Charles J. Haughey pursuant, to a request from the Tribunal of Enquiry, and Section 5 Of The Tribunal Of Inquiry Evidence Amendment Act 1979)

1. I was a member of Dail Eireann from June 1957 until November 1992. During that period of time I held the offices of Parliamentary Secretary to the Minister for Justice 1960-1961, Minister for Justice 1961 — 1964, Minister for Agriculture 1964 — 1966, Minister for Finance 1966 — 1970, Minister for Health and Social Welfare 1977 — 1979, TAOISEACH 1979 — 1981, 1982, 1987 — 1989, 1989 — 1992. I am a member of the Council of State. I am now aged seventy-one years and retired from public life.

2. Throughout my public life the late Desmond Traynor Chartered Accountant was my trusted friend and financial advisor. He was held in very high esteem in business circles and was widely regarded as a financial expert of exceptional ability. I never had to concern myself about my personal finances as Desmond Traynor took over control of my financial affairs from about 1960 onwards. He saw to it as his personal responsibility to ensure that I would be free to devote my time and ability to public life and that I would not be distracted from my political work by financial concerns. Mr. Traynor had complete discretion to act on my behalf without reference back to me. He arranged for the day to day management of my financial affairs and I never queried his expertise or the manner in which he handled them. Up to the end of 1990 Deloitte & Touche Chartered Accountants actually discharged my current liabilities in consultation with Mr. Traynor and in early 1991 Mr. Jack Stakelum took over

that responsibility. As part of the management of my finances Mr. Traynor would have had authority to raise bank or other borrowings. The arrangements which I had in respect of my personal finances was that my secretary would on a regular basis forward all invoices to Deloitte & Touche Chartered Accountants for payment and they would discharge these invoices from funds held by them as provided to them by Desmond Traynor. This arrangement continued until the end of 1990 when Jack Stakelum took over the arrangements in conjunction with Desmond Traynor.

3. I met Mrs. Margaret Heffernan on two occasions at Abbeville, Kinsaley. The first of these meetings took place in the summer of 1993. At the time it was not clear to me why Margaret Heffernan had called to see me. The greater part of our conversation was taken up with her describing to me the extreme difficulties Dunnes were experiencing because of the unpredictable and aggressive behaviour of her brother Bernard Dunne towards the other Directors. I may have said that it seemed to me from what she was saying that her brother was unstable on the basis of her account of what had been happening. To the best of my recollection she made only a brief reference to rumours of a payment to me from Dunnes. It was to the effect that she had been told by Mr. Irwin that Mr. Bernard Dunne had told him that he had paid to me £1 million. As far as I can recollect I would have said something along the lines that there are all sorts of rumours flying around and wild accusations and I could not be responsible for them or for what Mr. Irwin or Mr. Bernard Dunne might say in the high drama situation which followed Mr. Bernard Dunne's removal first of all from the chair and secondly as an Executive Director of Dunnes Stores. I was aware at the time of this meeting of a tense heated dispute between the various members of the Dunne family. I subsequently telephoned Desmond Traynor and told him what Margaret Heffernan had said. He replied that he was meeting Margaret Heffernan in a few days time and would hear what she had to say but that I need not be concerned about these rumours as they were without foundation.

4. I recollect meeting Mrs. Margaret Heffernan on the 5th day of November 1994 and I have read her evidence to the Tribunal in this regard. I accept her evidence in relation to what happened at this meeting but I am at a loss to understand her statement that I was extremely close to her brother Bernard Dunne from 1983 onwards. I note that Mrs. Heffernan cannot remember whether she instigated the meeting or not. There was no reference to any payment at this meeting. While my diary records a further meeting on 6th day of December 1994 I do not believe that this meeting actually took place.

5. In November 1994 I received correspondence from Matheson Ormsby Prentice, Solicitors acting on behalf of Dunnes Stores and I duly replied to same.

6. Desmond Traynor died in May 1994. At the funeral I was approached by Mr. Padraig Collery whom I did not know and who stated that he had taken over from Desmond Traynor. I had never met Padraig Collery before and had no knowledge of his business or profession. I never met with Mr. Collery other than this one brief meeting. After Desmond Traynor's death all invoices continued to be sent to Jack Stakelum and the arrangement with Mr. Stakelum continued.

7. Jack Stakelum would come to see me from time to time for the purpose of showing me financial statements.

8. As a result of the evidence adduced before this Tribunal and the documentation as furnished to me I now accept that the payments totalling £1.3 million as set out by the Tribunal were received for my benefit. I had no knowledge of the circumstances surrounding the payment of such monies but I accept the description as offered in evidence to this Tribunal by Mr. Noel Fox insofar as it touches upon the four payments totalling £1.1 million.

9. I dispute the evidence of Mr. Bernard Dunne that he called to Abbeville, Kinsaley, Co. Dublin on some date on or prior to the 30th of November 1991 and personally handed me three bank drafts of £70,000.00 each drawn on Rea Brothers in the Isle of Man on the account of Tutbury Limited. I say that no such meeting ever took place and Mr. Bernard Dunne is mistaken in his recollection in this regard. I never on any occasion received any of the three bank drafts referred to from Mr. Bernard Dunne nor from anyone on his behalf. Nor was I aware of their existence until Noel Smyth referred to them on 3rd February 1997.

10. Insofar as I accept that I received the benefit of the sum of £1.3 million as referred to herein I have seen the statement of evidence as prepared by Bernard Uniacke wherein he refers to a conversation with Mr. Bernard Dunne which allegedly took place on the morning of June the 15th 1993. I have no knowledge of either the subject matter or the content of that conversation. I neither introduced, initiated or brought about any change in fiscal or other legislation that would specifically affect either Bernard Dunne or Dunnes Stores Limited or any associated company.

11. On Friday 9th October 1992 I had dinner with Mr. & Mrs. Bernard Dunne and Mr. & Mrs. Noel Smyth in Abbeville, Kinsaley. This was my first meeting with Noel Smyth who I subsequently met on several occasions over the following years.

12. Noel Smyth telephoned me around the time the Lowry story broke in the newspapers at the end of November/early December 1996. He enquired if I had any information as to who was behind the leaking of the Lowry story to the newspapers and said that in his opinion that whoever was responsible was playing a very dangerous game. I informed him that I had

no idea whatsoever as to who was behind the story. Following my telephone conversation with Noel Smyth about the Michael Lowry newspaper story he subsequently telephoned me asking for a meeting and this was arranged for Saturday December 12th 1996 at 11.30 a.m.

13. Initially this meeting was arranged to take place in Abbeville, Kinsaley but at Mr. Smyth's request was changed to the home of a neighbour Noel Corcoran of "Emsworth".

14. At this meeting Noel Smyth showed me the Price Waterhouse Report and brought me through it. He pointed out that there was no reference to me personally in the Report. He showed me that there were references to my wife Maureen Haughey, my son Ciaran Haughey and my brother, Fr. Eoghan Haughey in the report.

15. A second meeting took place on Saturday 4th January 1997 at 11.00 a.m. in "Emsworth". My recollection is that Noel Smyth telephoned me prior to this meeting to arrange it. At this meeting Noel Smyth discussed the possibility of a Tribunal of Inquiry being established and what this would entail. I have a recollection that there was some talk about the Dunnes family litigation.

16. A further meeting took place on the afternoon of Monday 3rd February 1997 in my study in Abbeville.

17. My recollection is that on the morning of Monday 3rd February 1997 Noel Smyth telephoned me and stated that he had in his possession copies of three bank drafts in respect of which he said that Mr. Bernard Dunne had recently formed an impression that he may have handed them to me. I said this could not be so as I had never received them. I also indicated that I had no knowledge of any such bank drafts. He informed me that he had them in his possession and could he come out to see me to ascertain if I could be of any help in regard to them. I said it was fine for him to come out to Kinsaley and an arrangement was made that he would come out that afternoon. I did not ask Noel Smyth if I could revert to him regarding same. When Mr. Smyth arrived in Abbeville, Kinsaley he produced three copy drafts. I looked at them at his request and I was in a position to confirm that I had never seen them before and I had no knowledge of them. Mr. Smyth appeared to accept that this was the position and our meeting concluded. I deny that I indicated to Mr. Smyth that I had knowledge of these three bank drafts. Mr. Smyth did not ask me if I had lodged the drafts to my own account and I could not and did not reply to him in the negative nor could I or did I state that the drafts could be a source of some considerable embarrassment to me. I did not indicate to him that these drafts may have been lodged to an account associated with my accountant and financial advisor Mr. Desmond Traynor. I deny that I asked Mr. Noel Smyth if it was possible to get rid of or destroy the copy bank drafts which he had in question. I deny that Mr. Smyth indicated to

me or that there was any discussion regarding the fact that the bank drafts were themselves the subject matter of a Bankers Book Evidence Order or that Bernard Dunne would have to be informed of the fact that I Charles J. Haughey had received them or that as a result Bernard Dunne would be obliged to inform the Tribunal of this fact in due course.

18. I recall that a further meeting took place with Noel Smyth in Abbeville sometime later in the month of February 1997. I believe that this meeting was arranged by telephone at Noel Smyth's request. At this meeting Noel Smyth advised me very strongly to take the easy way out of all the tension and stress by going to the Tribunal and indicating that payments made to Desmond Traynor from Dunne sources had in fact been for my benefit. He stated that as there was no impropriety involved and as I had never sought these from or spoken to Bernard Dunne about them or granted any favours to Bernard Dunne or Dunnes Stores that I was in fact in no difficulty in regard to them. He stated that he realised that if I were to take this course of action it would possibly give rise to a tax liability and in such an event, Bernard Dunne would be prepared to provide £1 million to meet such eventuality. I rejected this offer and suggestion out of hand. I have no recollection of Mr. Smyth indicating to me that Mr. Dunne's offer in respect of £1 million was withdrawn and I doubt if such an event took place as I had totally rejected the offer as made by him on Mr. Dunne's behalf. I have never spoken about my place in history or in the community or anything of that kind to anyone. I do recall in the course of the conversation that Mr. Smyth enquired of me as to whether or not I had availed of the tax amnesty in 1993 and I informed him that I had not.

19. All these meetings as referred to with Mr. Noel Smyth were private but none of them were ever expressed to have been confidential between me and Mr. Smyth.

20. I never asked Mr. Bernard Dunne for any financial assistance or spoke to him about any matter concerning my financial affairs. I have no knowledge of any approach by the late Desmond Traynor to Mr. Bernard Dunne either directly or otherwise in respect of seeking financial assistance on my behalf. I have never had any discussion or communication with Mr. Noel Fox about my financial affairs or about any approach to Mr. Bernard Dunne for financial assistance.

21. In his evidence to the Tribunal Mr. Bernard Dunne referred to a number of meetings he had with me. Mrs. Margaret Heffernan in fact seems to refer to a larger number of meetings. Any meetings I had with Mr. Bernard Dunne were of a social nature and would have taken place predominantly after I had left office in February 1992. Before that my meetings with Mr. Bernard Dunne were very few.

22. I had a stock loan from ACC Bank for a number of years prior to 1987. The loan was used to stock the farm at Abbeville. Interest on this loan was I believe discharged on an annual basis and the loan continued thereafter. In 1987 I had been appointed Taoiseach and felt in the circumstances that it was inappropriate for me to maintain a loan account with a semi-state body. I discussed the situation with Desmond Traynor and he arranged for the discharge of the loan. Given the reasons for wanting the loan discharged I subsequently obtained written confirmation of the fact that the loan had been paid off. I had no knowledge of the source of the funds used to pay off this loan.

23. During the time I held public office I had no role in relation to the provision of security for Celtic Helicopters or to assist in its borrowings. From the documentation as furnished to me by the Tribunal it is apparent that Desmond Traynor used monies under his control to assist and to secure various borrowings for Celtic Helicopters. I was not aware as to whether or not such monies as used were funds which he was holding for me but clearly Desmond Traynor would have had authority to use funds held to my credit in this matter if he saw fit.

24. I am aware and accept that Mr. Bernard Dunne did make a contribution of £20,000 by way of a cheque on or about the 14th day of June 1989 in respect of election expenses. I was the ultimate beneficiary of Mr. Dunne's cheque which was lodged to the account of Maureen Haughey at The Educational Building Society, Malahide, Account number 13131516. This cheque in the first instance was handed to my wife on my behalf.

Dated this the 7th day of July 1997

Signed: *Charles J. Haughey*
          Charles J. Haughey

Eighth Schedule

Copy Statement of Mr. Charles J. Haughey dated 9th July 1997

Text of statement of Charles J. Haughey dated the 9th July 1997

"I wish to thank the Chairman for yesterday's adjournment. As a result of reviewing the excellent work of the Tribunal in considering the very helpful documentation recently received from Mr. Ben Dunne's solicitor, I now accept that I received the £1.3 million from Mr. Ben Dunne and that I became aware that he was the donor to the late Mr. Traynor in 1993 and furthermore I now accept Mr. Dunne's evidence that he handed me £210,000 in Abbeville in November, 1991.

In making this statement, I wish to make it clear that until yesterday I had mistakenly instructed my legal team. They have however agreed to continue acting for me for the duration of the Tribunal. I wish to thank them in this regard. I will give evidence to the Tribunal when required to do so."

Signed: Charles J. Haughey

Ninth Schedule

Copy statement of Charles J. Haughey dated 15th July 1997

1. I accept that I have not co-operated with this Tribunal in a manner which would have been expected of me. I deeply regret that I have allowed this situation to arise.

2. When I walked out of Government Buildings on February 11th 1992, I was determined to leave public life firmly behind me, to detach myself completely from it and to leave those who followed me free to manage things in their own way without any attempt by me to influence or interfere. The effect of this transition has been that my recollection of events became increasingly remote and diffused. In endeavouring to recall times, dates, the sequence of events, and details of meetings and conversations for the Tribunal I have been at this disadvantage.

3. I omitted to instruct my lawyers fully. It is against this background that I sent correspondence to the Tribunal and in particular, my letters of the 7th March 1997, 3rd April 1997, my statement of the 7th July of 1997 and Counsel's statement to the Tribunal on the 30th June 1997. These letters and statements were unhelpful to the Tribunal in the carrying out of its work.

4. I was concerned as to the effect that the publication of these payments would have for me in the public mind and in hindsight I accept that a lot of the problems and embarrassment that I have caused would have been avoided if I had been more forthcoming at each and every relevant period.

5. I would like to reiterate that I now accept that I received the £1.3 million from Mr. Ben Dunne and that I became aware that he was the donor to the late Mr. Des Traynor in late 1993 and furthermore I now accept Mr. Ben Dunne's evidence that he must have handed me £210,000 in Abbeville in November 1991.

6. I have absolutely no recollection of the November 1991 meeting, but it is clear from the evidence that the late Mr. Des Traynor received the money and that I got the benefit of it. I can offer no other rational explanation to show how the late Mr. Des Traynor could have received these drafts other than in the manner outlined by Mr. Ben Dunne and I am prepared to accept his evidence in this regard.

7. In 1993, subsequent to my departure from office, the late Mr. Traynor indicated to me that Mr. Ben Dunne had contributed in excess of £1 million to help him with my finances between 1987 and 1991 but I wish to emphasise that he had not told me this, while I was in office.

8. Throughout my public life the late Mr. Des Traynor was my trusted friend and financial adviser. He was held in very high esteem in business circles and was widely regarded as a financial expert of exceptional ability. I never had to concern myself about my personal finances. He took over control of my financial affairs from about 1960 onwards. He saw it as his personal responsibility to ensure that I would be free to devote my time and ability to public life and that I would not be distracted from my political work by financial concerns. The late Mr. Des Traynor had complete discretion to act on my behalf without reference back to me. In hindsight it is clear that I should have involved myself to a greater degree in this regard.

9. Mr. Dunne did not seek, nor was he granted, any favours. There is no improper motive associated with the payment of these monies. The Tribunal have had the opportunity of investigating and enquiring as to whether any actions or decisions of mine in Government were taken for the purposes or were motivated for the purposes of benefiting Dunnes Stores or otherwise than in the public interest. I will be bound by your judgement in this regard and I am confident that your findings will bear this out.

10. I apologise to you Mr. Chairman, the Tribunal team and to all concerned, but wish to emphasise that this serious lapse in the management of my personal affairs did not in any way affect the discharge of my public duty when in office.

Tenth Schedule

Payments to Streamline Enterprises

		Date	Amount
1.	Payment	14/11/88	£6,000.00
2.	Payment	13/12/88	£5,000.00 Stg.
3.	Payment	2/2/89	£9,945.00 Stg.
4.	Payment	25/10/89	£7,875.00 Stg.
5.	Payment	16/10/89	£7,950.00 Stg.
6.	Payment	19/10/90	£19,730.00 Stg.
7.	Payment	14/9/90	£15,825.00 Stg.
8.	Payment	3/9/91	£34,100.00 Stg.
9.	Payment	15/3/93	£55,314.00 Stg.

Eleventh Schedule

Extract from 1987 Audit Report of Ansbacher Cayman Limited

"GMCT have a large proportion of customers having "managed company" or "hold mail" status. In the former case GMCT provide directors or trustees for the client's company and has day to day control over the assets of the company in trust (although in normal circumstances the trustees act in accordance with the wishes of the undisclosed beneficial owner). These clients have a number of key characteristics:

(a) They are generally undisclosed except to the most senior manager of the company;

(b) The principals will not sign any documentation;

(c) The principals do not receive statements of account on a regular basis;

(d) The principals only occasionally (maybe once every two or three years) visit the company to review their affairs.

(e) Instructions are usually received by telex from solicitors or other trustees or by telephone from the principal. There is never any direct written instructions from the principal.

In view of the above there is a high risk of mismanagement or fraud and it is essential that strong controls are in place. From our review of Arthur Young's audit files it appears that controls in this area, are somewhat below best practice. In particular:

(a) There is only limited division of duties, and trust officers, as well as monitoring the accounts of the bank, also maintain the clients' accounts on behalf of the bank. To compensate for this lack of division of duties the Senior Directors review in detail every customer relationship annually.

(b) No attempt is made to obtain third party confirmation of balances or customer accounts. (Whilst principals may be reluctant to sign documentation/statements most institutions usually get the customers' solicitor or other representative to sign on the customer's behalf).

Local management consider the controls to be adequate and no action has been taken in respect of the above in view of the proposed sale."

110

Twelfth Schedule

Extract from 1989 Internal Audit Report of Guinness & Mahon (Ireland) Limited

"A matter of particular concern to us relates to the management and control of the Ansbacher Cayman deposits, amounting to nearly IR£38m and constituting almost 35% of the bank's liabilities. These deposits are under the sole charge of the Associate Director of the bank [Mr. Collery] who also acts, in practice but not officially, as a Dublin based representative of Ansbacher Limited and negotiates the rates with G & M in that capacity.

The Associate Director additionally manages the related anonymous off-shore "customer" deposits, on behalf of Ansbacher, almost entirely on his own without any evident accountability to the Board. In this respect too, he acts as a Dublin-based agent of Ansbacher whilst being a full-time employee of G & M. This dual role, which involves him in acting on behalf of both the parties to the transaction with little internal check not only creates serious conflicts of interest but also exposes the bank to unacceptable risks of fraud ...

Ansbacher Limited, a company based in Grand Cayman, has deposited, by way of call and fixed deposits, amounts equivalent to IR£38m with the bank ("Ansbacher deposits"). These deposits equate to funds lodged on off-shore call and fixed deposit accounts with Ansbacher Limited ("customer deposits") by Dublin-based customers.

The ledger accounting records of the customer deposits are maintained by the bank on a "bureau system" which shares the same hardware as, but is totally independent of, the IBIS/38 system of G & M, Dublin. Thus the Ansbacher deposits held in the bank's computer system are represented by the customer deposits held on the bureau system.

The bureau system is operated and controlled solely, on behalf of Ansbacher, by the Associate Director, Operations (DPC) and no other senior official of the bank has access to that system. Customer names are not held on the system but each deposit is identified by a code. We understand that DPC is aware of their names.

DPC deals direct with the customers or their agents. He negotiates calls/fixed deposit interest rates with them. He also negotiates, on behalf of Ansbacher Limited, with G & M dealers the rates payable on the Ansbacher deposits ensuring that the total interest received by Ansbacher Limited agrees with the total interest paid on the customer deposits. If the totals do not agree, adjusting entries are passed in the bank's books by DPC. We understand that

Ansbacher Limited is remunerated by way of a fee of 1/8% per annum calculated on the total deposits although we have not seen any legal documentation to this effect.

DPC also receives and processes the payment instructions in respect of customer deposits. The payments are in fact made from the Ansbacher deposits held in the bank's books. Corresponding book-keeping entries debiting customer accounts, which are technically offshore, are then made on the bureau system thus maintaining the equation of Ansbacher deposits with the customer deposits.

In practice (but not officially), therefore, DPC acts as a Dublin-based agent of Ansbacher Limited insofar as the management of customer and Ansbacher deposits is concerned, although he is employed full-time by the bank. All transactions relating to these deposits are initiated and processed by DPC. In addition to negotiating with both the parties to the transactions, he raises accounting entries and prepares input vouchers, deal slips etc. for both the parties (G & M and the customers of Ansbacher Limited). There is no internal check on his activity.

It should also be noted that standard controls generally applicable within the bank to call and fixed deposits are not applicable to Ansbacher deposits. For example, with respect to money market deals done with Ansbacher Limited, DPC, not the dealer, completes the deal slips; no counter party confirmations are received and the bank's outgoing confirmations are sent not to Ansbacher Limited but to DPC.

As mentioned before, DPC together with certain agent(s) of the customers, negotiates not only interest payable on the customer deposits but also interest payable on the Ansbacher deposits. This together with the ability to initiate and process payment instructions on the Ansbacher deposits with no effective internal check constitutes a serious control weakness. For example, interest rate negotiations could easily be manipulated so as to create a surplus of interest credited to Ansbacher call deposit accounts over the average interest payable on the corresponding customer call deposit accounts. As the function of maintenance and operation of the deposits is vested in one person only, the surplus may easily be misappropriated without detection because the equation of balances on customer deposits with the Ansbacher deposit will be maintained.

It should be pointed out that we have neither detected nor do we have any reason to believe that there has been any irregularity with respect to Ansbacher deposits. However, as the customer deposits constitute records of Ansbacher Limited (and not of G & M, Dublin) they have not been subject to our review. We have also not reviewed the procedures involved in opening up new customer deposits, if any new deposits are indeed taken. Further, we have not seen any mandate for the operation of the Ansbacher deposits and customer deposits.

In our opinion, lack of internal control over this activity coupled with the fact that the Ansbacher deposits constitute nearly 35% of the bank's liabilities expose the bank to serious risks of loss and embarrassment. These risks together with the legal position of the bank vis a vis the maintenance of offshore customer deposits by a bank employee and on the bank's premises need to be evaluated by the Board."